The Art of Teaching

The Art of Teaching

Big ideas, simple rules

Alan Haigh

PEARSON
Longman

Harlow, England • London • New York • Boston • San Francisco • Toronto
Sydney • Tokyo • Singapore • Hong Kong • Seoul • Taipei • New Delhi
Cape Town • Madrid • Mexico City • Amsterdam • Munich • Paris • Milan

Pearson Education Limited

Edinburgh Gate
Harlow CM20 2JE
Tel: 144 (0)1279 623623
Fax: +44 (0)1279 431059
Website: www.pearsoned.co.uk

First published in Great Britain in 2008

ISBN: 978–1–4058–7326–0

British Library Cataloguing-in-Publication Data
A catalogue record for this book is available from the British Library

Library of Congress Cataloging-in-Publication Data
Haigh, Alan.
    The art of teaching: big ideas, simple rules/Alan Haigh.
        p. cm.
    Includes index.
    ISBN-13: 978-1-4058-7326-0 (pbk.)
    1. Teaching. 2. Lesson planning 3. First year teachers-- Training of--
    United States. I. Title.
    LB1025.3.H327 2008
    371.102--dc22   2008000742

10 9 8 7 6 5 4 3 2 1
12 11 10 09 08

Typeset in Stone Serif 9pt by 3
Printed and bound in Great Britain by Henry Ling Ltd, Dorchester, Dorset

The publisher's policy is to use paper manufactured from sustainable forests.

Contents

section one ## Planning

section two **Behaviour and class management**

section four   # Assessment

It's priceless and it's free to all children – education!

Those who can – teach!

Prologue

This book is a 'starter', a survival guide. Hopefully it will help you reach a level of confidence and competence where you can begin to challenge yourself (instead of the children challenging you!), and then you will progress to a 'deeper' level of understanding about Teaching and Learning. Later in the book I discuss 'higher-order' teaching skills like 'deep-end' teaching and teaching children to think. In terms of Professional Development, three generic stages are recognised: Technical competence (acquiring the skills); Practical competence (applying the skills); and Reflective practitioner (a deeper level of understanding sometimes described as 'intuitive'). It is recognised that the deeper level is not always attained and is not normally achieved without considerable experience and intellectual engagement on behalf of the practitioner. (Professor Andrew Pollard's book or website: rtweb.net, on Reflective Practice is helpful here.)

This 'Art of Teaching' grew out of 30 years of both teaching children and training and educating students to teach. The majority were primary level but the same principles apply to the secondary phase too. The 'What's the Big Idea?' and 'It's not rocket science!' were two catch phrases that were plagiarised and used in my teaching to help students to focus. The reductionist philosophy ('Keep It Simple,' KIS) came from the struggle to explain complex scientific concepts to children and this seemed to transfer easily to the detailed expectations and understanding asked of new teachers.

The avoidance of reference to theory, research and literature has been deliberate, as this is intended as a practical guide to teaching and not for writing assignments. However, I hasten to add the old adage: 'Practice without Theory is static; Theory without Practice is sterile'. Theory and Research are essential to practice, but in my experience new teachers thirst for the practical and pragmatic first.

In line with my philosophy I have tried to make this book 'short and simple'. I hope I have succeeded. Please feel free to dip in and out of the book as required. Enjoy.

Alan Haigh
1 October 2007

Acknowledgements

I should like to thank all colleagues and children that I have taught with over the last 30 years from whom I have learned all that I know. In particular I should like to give special thanks to my wife Peggy Etchells, not only for her support and encouragement, but also for being a gifted teacher and Headteacher from whom I have learnt a great deal. Finally, I should like to acknowledge one of my PGCE students whom I supervised in a primary school in Ashbourne, Derbyshire, who kept telling me that my advice was better than anything she had read and I should write a book of my 'Big Ideas'.

Introduction

The philosophy of teaching through 'Big Ideas'.

This book is about the 'Big Ideas' that are behind the craft of
managing teaching and learning. The simplest ideas are the most
powerful. The principles of teaching are not age dependent, yet
learners do differ in their cognitive development and attitudes to
learning. This understanding of cognitive development has
moved on from Piaget's stage theory to a more sophisticated
understanding involving 'readiness to learn', growth and
maturation of the nervous system and crucially the recognition
of the power of teaching to enhance children's mental capacities.

The power of teaching through 'Big Ideas' is a unifying principle
that can be applied to the teaching of children of all ages as well
as to the training of their teachers. This principle holds together
the understanding of the pedagogy and the knowledge,
understanding and skills required by the curriculum. Piaget's
proposition that children learn by making sense for themselves
by internally adjusting the information they receive still holds
true. My proposition is that any approach to learning is better
facilitated by **beginning with the general** (Big Idea) and
deducing the particular. This approach provides the framework
into which people can fit the detail and make sense of the whole
for themselves. This works, in my experience, for the teaching of
teachers just as much as for the teaching of pupils and students.
The teacher has to make sense of the complexities of the
Planning, Teaching and Assessment in the same way that the
pupil has to master the complexities of the knowledge,
understanding and skills of the curriculum.

The above assertion that these principles are not age dependent
holds true, but the language, communication strategies and

pupil–teacher relationship vary with the age of the pupil. It is true to say that this book was written from the Primary teacher's perspective, but I have tried to base it on 'Big Ideas' that apply equally to Secondary teachers.

The first big idea is the principle of 'Big Ideas':

Big Idea:

Zoom out before you zoom in.

In a few words, look for the Big Idea that underpins what you are trying to teach. Whether it is your own practice or a concept you wish children to understand, step back for a moment and get a grasp of the bigger picture. It is analogous to 'fractals' (Mandelbrot 1975): as we pull back from a tiny piece of land and sea we recognise it is part of a bay, then part of a bigger coastline and then further back we recognise the country.

> **✱eg** You might introduce the physics of dynamics by saying that it is all about movement and what makes things move and what makes them stop moving, before any mention of Newton's Laws of Motion.

I believe that every subject, at every level, can be reduced to a set of 'Big Ideas' and these provide the essential constructs that we should begin with. What is more, we should represent these Big Ideas in everyday language that the audience can understand. Children do not readily recognise National Curriculum 'speak' when we are talking about learning objectives: similarly, scientific vocabulary is unfamiliar and also needs everyday language to make it comprehensible. This is not 'dumbing down', it is simply common sense. Once we have provided this foundation we can build in ever increasing levels of sophistication of language and thought.

*eg This book begins with the Big Idea that it is all about getting children to **sit down, be quiet and to listen and learn** and ends with another Big Idea that we want children to **enjoy and value their education and develop into independent lifelong learners.**

From this bigger picture I will begin to 'zoom in' and look at the lesser Big Ideas behind Planning; Behaviour and Class Management; Teaching, Learning and Assessment.

Planning

In an era of freebies with thousands of lesson plans on the Net and elsewhere, it is doubly important that new teachers understand the principles of lesson plan design so that they can use these resources and make them their own.

What do we teach our children?

The National Curriculum Programmes of Study set the legal framework and we should be further guided by the school's long-term and medium-term plans. The latest Primary National Strategy recommends greater curricular flexibility and the development of children as independent and autonomous learners.

chapter 1

Keep it as simple as ABC

A What do I want my children to learn?

B What do I want my children to do?

C How am I going to organise and manage it?

Decide on the lesson focus

Always start your planning with the 'A'; this is your lesson focus, which you can think of as the Lesson Objective. Too often beginners start their planning with 'B', which is what the children will do. This is understandable as they need to keep their children 'occupied' and they have seen or read about a good activity that seems appropriate. This could still be effective provided you derive the 'A' before you begin.

How do you do that? You simply ask yourself these two questions:

WHY are my children doing this?

WHAT are they going to learn?

If you can't answer these questions clearly and precisely then the learning will most probably not be achieved.

The 'B' is the vehicle that carries the learning. It doesn't always need to be 'whizzy' and exciting, but on the other hand it should not always be dull. It can range from the straightforward '1000 sums' to 'hands on investigations'. The best investigations are of course 'Hands on and Brains on', in other words doing and thinking.

The 'C' is probably the most difficult competence to acquire and, in my experience, the younger the children, the greater the difficulty. It can range from 'whole class' teaching to 'all singing and all dancing' integrated mixed-ability group work. How it is organised is up to the teacher's professional judgement and should be based on creating a balance between what is practical and what is in the best 'learning' interest of the children. The only guide I can give you is that if you use the 'whole class' approach all the time, then, unless you are exceptional, you are unlikely to achieve the intellectual engagement required for children's deeper understanding. On the other hand, if you engage in 'integrated mixed-ability group work' all the time, unless you are exceptional, it is unlikely that you will realise your learning objectives and, more importantly, you will burn yourself out!

Focus on one lesson objective at a time

When planning lessons we have to consult the National Curriculum Programmes of Study, which are the children's legal entitlement enshrined in the Education Reform Act 1988.

The Programmes of Study are made up of:

- **Knowledge** (facts, recall);
- **Understanding** (concepts, ideas);
- **Skills** (competencies, which must be practised to be acquired);
- **Attitudes** (values, to themselves, others, society – more about 'emotional wellbeing' than 'academic wellbeing'; however, ways of working and learning, and social behaviours are vital aspects of the attitudes in our hidden curriculum).

Remember: KUSA.

The Big Idea behind this strategy is to:

> Only focus the Lesson Objective (LO) on one of those variables at a time.
> Either K or U or S or A.

Why?

Because those different classifications of LOs generate different teaching strategies and classroom organisation. Most beginners can generate numerous LOs for a single lesson, but if you want your children to be clear about their learning then my advice is to choose *one* LO as priority and focus on that. If some children achieve other learning outcomes as well, then treat that as a bonus. (Keep It Simple; do one thing and do it right!) Decide whether the LO is mainly K, or mainly U, or mainly S, or mainly A, and plan and organise the lesson around that objective. (I did warn you that I was from the Reductionist/Simplistic School of Philosophy of Education!)

✳ eg It is a lovely summer's day and I decide to take the children on a short nature walk. A good idea, but what are they going to learn? Is it:

1 The names of some common flowers and trees which I know we will find. (Recognise; name and recall, i.e. **Knowledge**.)

2 That different plants are suited to growing in different places. (This is about the scientific concept of adaptation, i.e. **Understanding**.)

3 To practise their observation skills by looking more closely at leaves or flowers. (This is about observation, i.e. **Skill**.)

4 To appreciate the beauty and diversity in nature. (This is about appreciating and valuing nature, i.e. **Attitude**.)

Focus on one lesson objective. If, for instance, you choose the Knowledge aspect but the children also look more closely and appreciate the beauty and diversity, then you win, win, win and win. If you try to teach all four aspects at once, it is likely that many children will end up confused.

- **Knowledge lessons** are more straightforward. Looked at very simply, it is a case of tell, remember and recall. Often 'whole class', written and oral and mostly closed questions.

- **Understanding lessons** usually require children to explore and make sense for themselves with *your* help. Investigating, observing, discussing and questioning, which can be 'hands on' or can be text based or have a visual or oral stimulus. It can be whole class, group or individual. The key aspect of this process is the 'enquiry and dialogue' between teacher and children. This will involve much more 'open-ended' questioning and give children choices and seek reasoning.

(This involves a much deeper intellectual engagement from the children and is a more difficult lesson to plan and organise. See Section 3.)

■ **Skills lessons** on the other hand are much less challenging for the teacher. Most skills can be analysed and broken down into steps that children can practise, usually in a hierarchical order, until they have reached an acceptable level of competence. A sort of 'learning by numbers' military style. These lessons are often 'whole class', but can be group or individual and contain elements of demonstration and clear instruction.

✳ eg As seen on *Blue Peter*, (BBC TV) 'Here is one I made earlier!'.

■ **Attitude lessons** often involve raising awareness in children's minds, which informs their judgement and social and emotional behaviour. This is sometimes referred to as Values education. These lessons are similar in many ways to 'Understanding' lessons. They involve children 'making sense for themselves', with your help. Investigating, observing, discussing and questioning. It can be 'hands on' (scenarios/drama) or can be text based or have a visual or oral stimulus. It can be 'whole class', group or individual. The key aspects of this process are the 'enquiry and dialogue' between teacher and children. This will involve much more 'open ended' questioning and give children choices and seek reasoning. (Again, this involves a much deeper intellectual engagement from the children and is a more difficult lesson to plan and organise. See Section 3.) The dilemma when teaching 'Values' is whether to tell the children how to think and behave or teach them to decide for themselves, or both? Is it 'caught or taught'?

Question your proposed lesson outcome

Many lessons have one of three clear generic learning outcomes:

- the children will learn ...
- the children will be able to ...
- the children will understand ...

These lesson objectives are often common sense and provide the teacher and the children with clear learning intentions. However, you might sometimes find yourself with a teaching idea and proposed outcome but you are unclear about the lesson objective. In this case, if you question the outcome by asking *Why are my children doing this?* you will find that the answer can make the teaching and learning more meaningful to both teacher and children.

This strategy of testing your objective or outcome with this question can lead to the uncovering of a much 'Bigger Idea' which helps children make sense.

✳ eg Children in Y6 may be taught the different technical elements of persuasive language and writing (NC KS2; En3 9c).

Why are my children doing this?
Perhaps the idea that persuasion and reason are more effective than force or throwing tantrums could be more motivating for children to learn, not to mention a vital interpersonal life skill!

Relating where possible our everyday teaching to the bigger picture motivates and helps children to make sense. Knowing why you are doing something may not make it less boring, but the rationale may make it more acceptable. Many teachers use this process instinctively and always try to put the learning in a meaningful context for their children. The suggestion here is that using one simple question will help new teachers clarify the learning for themselves and their children.

Don't lead children down dark tunnels

Lesson objectives outline what we want our children to learn, as we have discussed above. This learning is the curriculum which is principally to be found in the National Curriculum Programmes of Study and DfES guidance. There are also very important lesson objectives that are taught through the 'hidden curriculum', such as Values education; Emotional wellbeing; Thinking and Behaviour. (The 'hidden curriculum' means the aspects of the curriculum that are not laid down in the Programmes of Study but are equally important for our children to live and learn.)

Some teachers use the acronyms:

> WALT: We Are Learning To, to make their lesson objective clear
> and
> WILF: What I am looking For, to make their expectations clear.

As someone once said to me, 'Don't lead children down dark tunnels'; tell children what you want them to learn, show them how to go about it and what it should look like.

Try to use 'child speak' not 'National Curriculum speak' by putting it into language that the children will understand. Give children the 'big picture' first (place the learning in context) and then show them where they are going and how to get there.

✳ eg 'Today we are going to learn how to make our stories more interesting by choosing more exciting and interesting words.'
(NC 'speak' KS1; En3 1a: 'use adventurous and wide ranging vocabulary'.)

It will help them to make sense of their learning and begin to construct meaning. As we have said before, if *you* are clear about the learning objective, then the children will also be clear, and this will give your lesson structure, focus and direction. Remember, most children can only get their head around one thing at a time and that is why it pays to Keep It Simple.

Give the lesson a beginning, a middle and an end

The **Lesson Structure** is the content and chronology of the lesson – in simple terms the 'beginning, middle and end', which should be decided by the teacher after considering the children's abilities and the curriculum content. One size definitely does not fit all!

- The **beginning** is the introduction and context.
- The **middle** contains the 'teaching points'.
- The **end** of the lesson needs to summarise and consolidate the learning and is sometimes referred to as the plenary.

Plenaries need not be restricted to the ends of lessons; this strategy can be used to summarise during the lesson or at the end of a series of lessons.

Make links to previous learning

Wherever possible make links to previous knowledge and experience. This means not only previous lessons in that subject so as to recap on the knowledge or process previously covered, but also knowledge of other subjects that are associated with it and may provide a meaningful context at the beginning of the lesson. Sometimes analogy and modelling using other subjects provides a good 'advance organiser' for the children. On other occasions you may be able to make links to the children's own experiences outside school.

> **✳eg** NC KS2; Sc2 4a: to make and use keys.
>
> 'When we went pond dipping we saw lots of creatures whose names we didn't know. Today we're going to learn a way of identifying what they are called from the way they look. It's a bit like a picture dictionary where you can find out the name of something by looking for its picture. Only here we're going to ask questions about how our pond creatures look one step at a time until it leads us to the right picture.
>
> For instance, Has it got legs? 'Yes' will take us to pictures of pond creatures with legs and 'No' will take us to pictures of pond creatures without legs. We can then ask another question to lead us to the answer (rather like a detective). For example, if the answer is 'Yes' then we could ask, 'Has it got six legs?' and this might finally lead us to a picture of a pond skater like this one.'

It is about using common sense and making connections that children can grasp in order to link ideas and previous learning.

chapter 2

Plan to teach with precision

Use small steps

Break the lesson down into small steps and create a **learning pathway**. More able children run down the path or take several steps at the same time; other children proceed at their own speed. The beauty is that you know where they are all going and how far down that road they are. KIS!

In order to create this pathway you need to deconstruct the learning objective into logical steps or sequences. Each of the steps will have a mini learning objective, which I shall refer to as a **teaching point**.

They then address the 'B', i.e. what the teacher and the children will be doing at these points in order to achieve the mini learning objective. This gives the lesson not only structure, but coherence and a clear direction. When a lesson has all of these three elements it is not difficult to maintain pace.

＊eg If my lesson objective was to give the children some understanding of the causes and consequences of the 2007 floods in South Yorkshire and Humberside (NC KS2; Geog Theme 6c: water and its effects), then I would need to deconstruct the lesson objective and plot my teaching points:

1 Water is part of a natural (re)cycle

2 Water goes downhill (gravity)

3 Water is heavy and has huge force

4 Low-lying land and housing are at risk

All you need to do now is decide what you will say and what the children will do at each point. You can make the lesson as simple or as complex as necessary to suit the children's age and ability.

This was a simple example of constructing a sequence of teaching to keep both you and the children on track.

Teaching points are the point of teaching

As you can see from the above a teaching point is a sub-set of the learning objective. This is what the teacher will reinforce as s/he goes through the lesson, and this gives the teaching a certain precision as opposed to vagueness. The teacher is much more focused on what s/he is going to praise and emphasise and knows when to move on to the next point. Further they provide an 'aide mémoire', not only for the teacher but also for the children. If you write up on the board the key teaching points for the children as you go along, you can use them in the plenary to reinforce, clarify and consolidate the learning.

There is no simple answer to the question: 'How many teaching points should there be for one lesson objective?' In general, the fewer the better, but it depends on the difficulty of the content and the ability of the children. Between three and six key points are usually manageable in most lessons, though it is not written in stone.

Most children are limited in how much they can take on board at one time. Precision teaching enables the teacher to provide a solid platform from which the children can jump off and explore for themselves. In one sense it is direct teaching but it can be very creative and pave the way for much more independent learning.

Consolidate and make links to future learning

In the same way that we made links to previous learning at the beginning, then, if at all possible, at the end we should recap and try to link forward. This doesn't just mean link to the next lesson; we could also link to other subjects and the implications on the children's own experiences outside school.

*eg Previously we mentioned 'adventurous and wide-ranging vocabulary', which could be linked to work on adverbs and adjectives or *The Jabberwocky* by Lewis Carroll.

Or

The work on binary keys for pond creatures could lead not only to plant identification and use of flora but also to how fault-finding manuals work.

chapter 3

Don't just download

Customise your lesson plans

Don't just download, make lesson plans your own. No two teachers teach in exactly the same way, nor should they.

The National Curriculum Programmes of Study are the legal entitlement of our children. (N.B. The Literacy and Numeracy strategies are advisory and, unlike the NC, are not enshrined in law.) To an increasing extent, much of our planning is produced 'one step removed' from the Programmes of Study, as pre-prepared lesson plans in one form or another. They can be downloaded from the QCA; Teachernet; commercial sites or your own school or LEA intranet. These are valuable labour-saving devices; nevertheless we need to question them and give them our ownership so that we are more comfortable when we use them. We need to explore the learning objective, so that we can then plan the learning pathway suitable for our class.

If *we* are clear about the planning, it is more likely that the children will be clear about what they are learning and doing. We are not doing this for the sake of it, but to test the planning against our own thinking and match it to the needs of our class. In fact, the plan may need very little change, but that process of examination is vital for our understanding of someone else's thinking, and in the absence of being able to question them we need a **methodology.**

Use a lesson plan methodology

Let's look at an example. I have chosen Unit 1E: 'Pushes and Pulls' from the Schemes of Work on the Standards Site (DfES), because they are heavily used, and Science in particular, because it is often more difficult for teachers to recognise the scientific principles involved. It is important to appreciate that this lesson planning methodology is generic and can be applied to all subjects at any level.

The six steps can be used from Early Years teaching to teaching Higher Education students.

Methodology

Unit 1E: Pushes and Pulls

Step 1 Deconstruct the learning objective(s)

Simply ask yourself, 'What's the Big Idea'? Consider what you think it means, i.e. what do I want my children to learn from this?

The *why* question is what we need in order to test any proposed teaching. Simply ask yourself, 'Why are my children doing this? What will they learn from this? Is that what I want them to learn from this?' Analyse and then synthesise the learning objective in words that are appropriate for your children; remember to focus on one LO at a time.

(N.B. The learning objective suggested by the original planner may be acceptable as it is. Do not change things for the sake of changing things!)

There are three objectives given in Unit 1E:

- That pushing or pulling things can make objects start or stop moving.

- To identify similarities and differences between the movement of different objects.

- To make suggestions about how objects can be made to move and to find out whether they were right.

Ask the *why* question to determine the real lesson objectives. In other words: What are the Big Ideas behind these suggestions? What are they asking my children to learn?

Here are examples of some of my thoughts:

- The concept of **cause** and **effect**, a basic tenet of science.

- The concept of a **force**. Nothing moves unless something makes it, even if you cannot see it, e.g. wind.

- The amount of push or pull will affect how things move or stop moving (**energy**).

- We are also asking children to begin the process of 'testing their hypotheses'. In ordinary language, this means making guesses about what they think will happen and testing to see if they were correct (**scientific enquiry**).

We are, believe it or not, looking at Newton's Laws of Motion, but I wouldn't dream of saying that. We are also beginning to get our Y1 children to start to think using Scientific Method (you might recognise this as Sc1: Scientific Enquiry), but I wouldn't tell them that either!

Step 2 Prioritise your learning objective(s)

Now we have deconstructed, let's decide how many lessons we want and which lesson objectives will take priority.

This is entirely up to the teacher; there is no need to follow a prescription in the NC Curriculum Guidance as long as you are delivering the appropriate learning objectives linked to the Programmes of Study. If you want to check, look at the Programme of Study or look at the QCA's simpler breakdown of KS1 or KS2 by subjects and areas covered, on their website (qca.org.uk). For coverage for Years 1 and 2, it says: Scientific Enquiry for Sc1 and Forces for the requirements for Sc4. This corresponds well with our thoughts in the box at the end of Step 1 above.

If you want the lesson to concentrate on Scientific Enquiry, then that is your focus and that is the lesson objective that you choose, in other words the fourth of our thoughts above about children learning to test their hypotheses.

 Children playing and exploring; finding things out; trying to make sense of them; making predictions encouraged by your 'what would happen if?' type of question.

Any other learning that occurs, for example about the physics of Forces or how to capture and report their findings, will be a bonus. We are not teaching these objectives in this lesson, so don't try. Concentrate on the sub-set of the 'Testing Hypotheses' objective, e.g. Observation; Raising Questions and Testing to see if they are right.

Earlier we advocated using an 'advance organiser' and 'child speak', like the example below.

'We are going to explore which of our toy vehicles moves the best.'

Use your own words but make them child-friendly and give the children a picture of what you are looking for – an 'advance organiser'.

At the end of the lesson, in the plenary, you will need to emphasise the real learning objective, which is the way they thought and acted in order to find out things for themselves, and tell them that this is what scientists do when they want to find things out (Scientific Enquiry: Sc1).

However, if on the other hand you want them to learn about the physics of Forces and Movement (SC4), that is a different lesson and a different lesson objective.

You might design a lesson for children to discover about the effects of motion, direction and the size of the force
or
a lesson on how to move things more easily (size, mass, friction etc.).

Step 3   Identify the lesson focus

Is it Knowledge, Understanding, Skills or Attitudes?

Identify the type of lesson that is required. This will affect the planning and organisation of the lesson and help you to make it more appropriate to the needs of your class.

We decided above on the 'Scientific Enquiry' lesson objective, which will involve teaching children a way of thinking and working. This is probably an Attitude and process of working.

This lesson objective is about introducing children to the process of scientific enquiry; it is a general lesson objective to give children the 'Big Idea' behind working scientifically. It is an example of the 'bigger picture' which should precede all our units of teaching, whatever the subject, because children learn better if they move from the general idea to the particulars of that idea. We shall learn more about this in Section 3, Teaching and Learning.

To teach children the whole of the NC SC1 (Scientific Enquiry), you would need to follow this lesson with individual lessons on observation; raising questions; making predictions; testing hypotheses; recording and interpreting results etc. (For more details look up *Primary Science: Taking the plunge* by Wynne Harlen.) This approach to teaching will allow you to begin to 'zoom in', as mentioned in the Introduction, and teach the sub-set of learning objectives, that is the particulars that make up the 'bigger picture'.

Step 4   Decide on the teaching points

Break down the chosen learning objective of introducing Scientific Enquiry to the children into a series of teaching points.

What are the key teaching points?

∗eg

- Looking carefully and talking about it (observation), e.g. Which toy vehicle do you think will be the fastest?

- Encouraging children to be curious and raise questions (hypothesising), e.g. Why do you think the sports car will be quicker than the lorry?

- Encouraging children to put their curiosity to the test (fair testing), e.g. How can we test them to find out?

- Encouraging children to make sense of what they have seen (explain their results), e.g. Why do you think the lorry was the best?

Please note that the task was engineered by the teacher to produce an unexpected result. Most children will choose the sports car, but a little surprise teaches them to be more careful when jumping to conclusions.

Step 5   Decide on the learning activities

Decide for each teaching point what the teacher will do and say and what the children will do. The example above will give you the simple idea. You will then need to differentiate as and when necessary to cater for the different abilities in the class.

Step 6   Decide how you are going to resource and organise the lesson

Now we have got this far, the activities and resources almost decide themselves. Our lesson objective is to encourage children to work in a more scientific way and in particular to observe and then raise questions involving movement, (pushes and pulls) and then to test them. We could use anything such as: toy cars; blow football, a roller skate, a ball, a brick etc. Take your pick.

Next decide how you are going to organise the different parts of the lesson to follow your learning pathway from the beginning, through the middle, to the end of the lesson. You need to choose that which will suit you and your class best – from whole class teaching to group work and individual work; from work sheets and cards to children writing up independently.

＊eg

- Introduction of the idea of looking carefully to see which is the best and then testing it:
  Whole class teaching, e.g. instructing, explaining, demonstrating, modelling, etc.
- Reporting on their observations:
  Whole class mini-plenary to make the first two teaching points and draw out some of the questioning and curiosity

the children have shown and then to challenge them to find out which is the best.

- Exploring how they could find out which was the best: Group work, e.g. activity sheets with resources and suggestions on their tables.

- Plenary:
Whole class: Draw out the learning about how scientists work and reinforce the four key teaching points you identified in Step 4 and put them on the board or project them using the computer.
Further, make links to the next lesson, e.g. How can we make a vehicle move faster? This will be further practice and reinforcement of working as scientists do.

If you want to test the success of your lesson, say to yourself, 'What do the children know now that they did not know before the lesson started?' Then try asking them and see if it matches what you thought.

chapter 4

Differentiate to accommodate

Analyse the range of abilities

What is differentiation? No, it is not the dreaded mathematics of calculus! It is common sense, and simply means that you should try to vary the degree of difficulty of the work to match the range of abilities in the class. Easier said than done! One thing you cannot do is to individualise the work for each child.

Generally speaking your class will fall into three clusters (able, more able and less able); you should be able to recognise these clusters quite quickly, though there may be a variance between subjects, so keep an open mind. There may also be some 'outliers', as they say in statistics; these will be the children with learning difficulties and the gifted and talented children, who will probably need special tasks prepared for them.

Decide on differentiation by outcome or by task

Normally we differentiate in two ways – by outcome and by task.

> ***eg** **By outcome**: same task and starting point, but some children will progress further and faster and finish at a different point. A very simplistic example of this principle would be a piece of art work or a PE skill. All the children would do the same thing but the individual outcomes would be different.

> ***eg** **By task**: different tasks and/or starting points matched to the ability of the different groups. A common example of this would be in numeracy where, after introducing the main lesson and teaching and explaining to the whole class, you would set different work for different groups of children, from the more able to the less able.

This is a challenge to all teachers, not just to new teachers. Experience is essential in planning and managing differentiation and every class is slightly different. The good news is that the same common sense principles apply:

Begin with the simplest form of differentiation, i.e. by outcome, and make sure you have some extension work for the quicker finishers.

Plan extension work for early finishers

Inevitably some children will finish more quickly than others and will need extra work to keep them occupied. The one thing you can't afford to do is begin to teach the quicker finishers a new skill or concept at this time. (This should be left to a new lesson which will need preparing for.)

The principle is to extend the lesson using the skills, knowledge and concepts the children already have. The simple answer is to give the children more of the same, for example do another page. This can be satisfactory but can lead to death by a thousand sums!

It is better if you can make the extension work more challenging, something that OfSTED is always looking for. You can achieve this by taking the concept or skill or knowledge they have just learned and setting them a problem to solve or further research to do. 'So how could we find out if?' or 'Can you find another way/explanation?' or 'Very good, see how you get on with this.' (In true *Blue Peter* style you have already prepared a work sheet for this occasion.)

For emergencies it always pays to have a set of 'plan Bs' in reserve in case the lesson doesn't work or the children finish too soon. A colleague of mine used to have a set of 10-minute activities, from an Alan Ahlberg poem to a number puzzle, for just such a situation.

chapter 5

Integrate to stimulate

What is meant by the terms Thematic, Topic or Integrated Planning? This is where the learning involves cross-curricular links between subjects, allowing us to teach subjects outside their lesson slots. This approach is normally seen in Primary schools but can sometimes be observed in early years of secondary schools.

It is refreshing for both children and teachers, particularly at the end of a busy term. It can be done as a whole afternoon's activity throughout the week or even a whole week's activity where the normal timetable has been completely suspended, or as a whole school focus for a week. The duration and depth of integration will depend on the medium-term planning decided by the teaching team. In the 1970s some schools organised all their teaching in this way; it was known as the 'integrated day' and was an offspring of the Plowden Report. This is a very demanding approach to planning and only successful in the hands of accomplished practitioners. Once again my advice would be to Keep It Simple. Begin with limited topic time and integrate the curriculum over just a few subjects.

The 'Three Wise Men' Report of the 1990s, (*Curriculum Organisation and Classroom Practice in Primary Schools*, Alexander, Rose and Woodhead, 1992) was one of the factors that led to the demise of topic work and the narrowing of the primary curriculum. The report quite rightly pointed out that much topic work was mind-numbingly dull, with children copying large tracts from reference books and drawing and colouring. However, in another section they did point out that, when topic work was done well, it was one of the most effective and enjoyable ways of teaching and learning. Unfortunately the damage was done and this statement was ignored by the Government of the day.

Fortunately, *A Vision for Teaching and Learning in 2020* (DfES 04255–2006DOM–EN) talks about flexibility and says:

> 'For example, the time required for each subject is not statutory and there is no requirement that curriculum content should be taught in subject blocks.' (p. 18)

Make obvious links to other subjects

The Big Idea is that some aspects of subjects make natural links with other subjects and would make more sense to the children if taught simultaneously.

There are some DON'Ts:

- Don't contrive links. There was a school of thought at one time which advocated that the whole curriculum should be integrated into the topic. (Personally I always had problems linking the topic of 'Trees' with PE!)

- Don't make links unless common sense tells you they will make sense to the children.

- Don't use all the links that you brainstormed in the original planning. Be selective, it is quality not quantity.

The QCA have good advice and suggestions on their website (Customise your curriculum), where they talk about embedding; adapting units and combining units. However, you must develop a planning methodology that puts the learning as first priority, and not just the construction of a creative topic masterpiece.

Use a topic planning methodology

As with our lesson planning process, we need a topic planning process, a **methodology**.

We need to ask ourselves those key questions again:

Why am I doing this?
and
What do I want my children to learn?

From a philosophical standpoint:

- It is more enjoyable to learn in this way;
- It allows children to exercise much more independence;
- It encourages research skills;
- It encourages thinking and decision making.

However, what are they going to learn with respect to the Programmes of Study is the vital question that the methodology must also answer. This will depend on what stage the class has reached at this time, what they have done, what you wish to reinforce and what new learning you need to introduce. As has been said before, use a deductive thinking process, i.e. start from the 'big picture' (general) and then work down from aims to lesson objectives (particulars).

How do I decide on the 'big picture'?

Here are examples of two approaches.

✱eg **Subject centred**: English, Maths, Science, History etc.

Theme centred: rather than an emphasis on the Knowledge aspect, we are often drawing more on the Skills and Attitudes aspects of the Programme of Study and our 'hidden curriculum'.

Subject centred

■ Take the subject you need to concentrate on at this time, e.g. History, KS2. What are the Big Ideas? They are laid out for us in the programmes of Study or the QCA versions, e.g. chronological understanding; knowledge of events in the past; historical enquiry etc.

■ Choose your overall aim, e.g. an understanding of the change over time of the peoples of these British Islands, through the topic of 'Invaders'.

This is an attempt to give an historical perspective of invasion and conquest prior to other more detailed studies of different periods.

The historical perspective of conquest will be the continuity strand that will make the topic coherent. The history is obvious, from Romans through to Victorian Britain.

We are not concerned with detail, just chronology and characteristic features of the periods (NC Programme of Study (PoS) for History; KS2 2a).

■ Brainstorm the links.

Place 'Invaders' in the *centre* of your plan and then plan *outwards* to identify your subject lesson objectives.

Look at other subjects and what is appropriate for your class/year group at this time in the medium-term plans or NC PoS/QCA.

> **✱ eg** Y3 Maths: Counting and understanding numbers: 'Read, write and order whole numbers to at least 1000 . . . and rounding up to nearest 10 or 100 etc.' (DfES Standards Site, Primary Framework for literacy and mathematics.) This should make sense when superimposed on our time line from 0–2007; never mind the negative numbers BC.
>
> Y3 Geography: Knowledge and understanding of places and why they were there (3e KS2 PoS). Regions, towns and rivers etc.

Here is an example of how brainstorming might begin.

MATHS	SCIENCE	ENGLISH
Number 1000	Building materials of	Poetry of the periods
Place value	the periods	
Distances		

INVADERS

GEOG	ART	MFL
Regional rivers	Jewellery design	French from
Towns, hills	of the periods	Norman times

This is a simple outline; the real challenge is to keep it manageable in the time available. Try to remember that it is quality not quantity, no matter how enthusiastic you are or how much you know about the topic.

Theme centred

■ Take the theme you wish to focus on and place it centre stage. It could be anything that permeates the curriculum, hidden or otherwise, for example Key aspects of learning across the curriculum (DfES Primary National Strategy, 0524–2004G): Problem solving; Working with others; Reasoning etc. or Financial capability; Enterprise education; Education for sustainability (National Curriculum: About Key Stage 1 and 2, p. 22).

■ We could take as an example Managing Money and work out the Big Ideas and see where they touched our subjects and curriculum objectives, that were appropriate for our Y6 children at this time.

Here is another example of how brainstorming might begin.

SAVING	BORROWING
Banks; PO;	Moneylenders;
Money boxes;	Debt;
Credit Unions	Interest charges

MONEY

EARNING	SPENDING
Pocket money;	Budgeting;
Jobs;	Credit cards
Child labour	

This can be a fun way of working, one that is very creative and enjoyable. One of the advantages is that we can cover the basic curriculum without the children realising it because of the nature of the applied knowledge. I will not fill in the details but I am sure you can see endless possibilities from Dickens, to money maths, to RE, to history, to the modern-day scourge of many families – debt and poverty.

■ Create a curriculum balance matrix.

The next thing we have to do is to record the curriculum balance to ensure that the coverage is reasonable and appropriate for the Y6 learning objectives in the PoS. A simple matrix will do the trick.

	Maths	Science	English	History	RE	PSHE
Week 1	£s/euros	Metal	Dickens	Coins	Jesus	Debt
Week 2	Income Expenditure		Shylock			
Week 3	Interest charges				Islam	

The rows tell us the lesson objective condensed into one word, e.g. Jesus refers to the morality of the moneylenders in the Temple and Islam refers to their law against charging interest.

The columns show the progression either by lesson or by the week, according to your time frame. Once again it is nice to have a Big Idea to reinforce and give the topic coherence; for example, in this case it could be; 'manage money sensibly' or 'neither a borrower nor a lender be': The lessons will almost plan themselves now you are clear about the topic objectives.

Think about your title

Sometimes the topic titles themselves can restrict our thinking and planning; on the other hand they can also have the opposite effect.

Convergent titles: tend to be those that focus on a main subject input, such as *Invaders* (History) or *Shape* (Maths) or *Growth* (Science) or *Water* (Science and Geography).

Divergent titles: tend to be those that permeate the curriculum more easily and set off a chain reaction of links, e.g. *Money* or *Change* or *Movement*. (The challenge here is to control the growth to stop the topic becoming unmanageable and to keep the learning focused.)

Plan creatively with discipline

Discipline here refers to your thinking. As has been mentioned before, you can't take a 'laissez faire' attitude towards the process and make wonderful but esoteric links. We must be mindful of our aim and the supporting objectives and make sure that they are appropriately embedded in the curriculum that is appropriate for our children. We must examine our brainstorm and curriculum balance and cross-check with the NC Programmes of Study for the appropriate age. Hopefully, if we have followed the school's long-term and medium term plans we should need very little pruning or alteration.

What I have tried to do above is to give you a planning rationale for topics, a **methodology**. There are many ways of planning topics and above are two examples of contrasting ways, one within the subjects and one outside the subjects. The challenge with planning topics is not what you put in, but what you leave out! Teachers used to be full of creativity and a thousand ideas; perhaps the time for teachers to think like this has come again, thank goodness!

chapter 6

Don't teach everything to the same depth

What do I do about overload?

There is too much to teach and things are being added all the time and not much is taken away. Common sense tells us that we need to prioritise to meet the needs of our class. We need to start from the simple and work up to the complex: quality not quantity.

The Big Idea here is that:

We do not have to teach everything to the same depth.

There are 'light touches' and 'heavier touches'; the skill is the teacher's professional judgement which is required in order to meet the Programmes of Study (legal entitlement); the needs of the children, and the curriculum priorities identified by the school.

The main emphasis has to be on the curriculum demands, which are 'measurement driven', i.e. subject to testing, and this must be thoroughly addressed whether we like it or not. However, not all the knowledge and understanding needs to be taught to the same depth to comply with 'coverage' and this again is the teacher's professional judgement based on the knowledge of the curriculum and the needs of the class.

 There are also peripheral strategies, which can be covered with lighter brush strokes and which can add further interest and enjoyment for both you and the children.

e.g. using story; music; art; a walk, and even some science or history!

Behaviour and class management

chapter 7

Get children to sit down, be quiet and listen to you

Until you can get children to sit down and listen quietly, you will not be able to teach them to any great effect. This seems like stating the obvious, but the obvious sometimes needs stating so that we can deconstruct it and identify the strategies needed to achieve our objectives. We have to start as we mean to go on, which means that we have to establish our 'classroom presence' as soon as possible.

Establish your classroom presence

The above is once again a simple statement of the obvious, but we ignore it at our peril. Here is some advice.

Look smart, be prompt and be prepared

- The expected image of a teacher is a conservative one of sobriety and sensibleness and our dress should reflect that. You may choose to wear adventurous leisure attire, but torn jeans and low-cut tops and hipsters are not normally appropriate for the classroom.

- Always be in the classroom before the children and stand tall at the front of the class. Be there to greet them with a smile and a 'good morning' and the occasional stern look or gentle reprimand. This sends the clear 'I'm in charge message' before you start.

- **Tell the children that you will be teaching them** for the next 'x' weeks. Not 'I will be taking you..'. Establish your teaching credentials. You are a teacher, regardless of the fact that you may be a student. If they ask you if you are a student, don't hesitate, look them straight in the eye and say that is correct and add I am a *beginning* teacher and will soon be having a class of my own. Avoid the use of the word 'student'; it has certain connotations even with primary children.

- **Insist and persist until you have silence.** Ask politely and assume the request will be followed and use a firm and strong voice.

✳eg 'Quiet please! Thank you!' followed by hard stares of disapproval where necessary.

Teachers of young children have routines for the children to follow: from counting back from 5, to hand signals and gestures. These are known as 'distracters', sounds or movements that break the children's absorption with themselves and their friends and refocus them on the teacher. You must remember that most children do not deliberately ignore their teacher: they are often jostled, disturbed and excited by being thrown into a mix of 30 other children and are busy trying to establish their own position and boundaries to feel safe. An important part of the teacher's job is to provide that safety. (See Chapter 11.)

- **Teachers need to maintain objectivity**, which is not always easy when the nature of the job involves a personal and caring relationship with all our children. However, the children do need to recognise when the teacher means business. The voice and attitude of the teacher change to a more serious mode and we establish the facts of the matter and then proceed to make our judgement and explain this to the children in a calm, clear manner.

- **Practise your repertoire of voices** and use them consistently. These are the behaviour clues and signals that the children have to interpret, so they must be clear. There is obviously the open and smiling, encouraging teacher voice and body language; at the other extreme there is the disapproving stiff body posture, sharp look and slow staccato language using a lower pitch of voice to send out warning signals. There is also a range of half-way steps between the two ends of this spectrum that you will need to perfect. You should avoid the sudden change from 'accelerator to brake' teaching style that would result from just using the extremes of the voice spectrum.

- **Eye contact:** look directly at the child you are speaking to and engage their eyes. Your eyes can smile or look cross. If you are speaking to the whole class then hold your eye contact in different areas of the room for 5–10 seconds at a time and let all the children know that you have them in view.

 I personally am a very 'right sided' person and tend to have a blind spot on my left, the segment on the clock face from 30–40 minutes past the hour. As a result I can ignore the 4 or 5 children in this area without realising it. To correct this you need to move your position (or the children's), so that all the children are in your viewing arc, which is from 20 minutes past the hour to 20 minutes before the hour.

- **Provide early success** by planning the first day in detail with all the resources ready and on hand. Use a 'direct' mode of teaching using mainly 'whole class' teaching. Give the children straightforward tasks with curriculum they are familiar with. Make sure you explain to children that they are beginning with easier work but will be progressing to more challenging work later in the week. Make sure that after the first lesson you tell them how pleased you are with them and at the end of the day you repeat the congratulations.

This is the first step on a journey of establishing a confidence that comes from knowing what you are doing and how you are going to do it, and establishing a warm and caring classroom ethos where children appreciate that they are there to work and learn and you are there to teach and help.

The Big Idea is to establish your position of authority without being authoritarian.

chapter 8

Set clear boundaries and guidelines

Establish clear expectations of work and behaviour

Children need to know the 'rules of the game', have them explained and know what is acceptable and what is not. You then need to focus on reinforcing them positively (praise), as soon as you see them being followed (*Operant conditioning* B.F. Skinner). The same psychology applies not only to their social behaviour but also to their academic behaviour.

The Big Idea here is that:

> Teachers manipulate the children's behaviour by rewarding the behaviour they wish to see.

Easier said than done, but it does work; you need to be *persistent* and *consistent*!

Bad behaviour can't be ignored. Only punish as a last resort and escalate the sanctions carefully. Begin with something like: 'Some of us are forgetting our rule' or 'I think we need to try a little harder to . . .'. (See Chapter 12.)

Use a simple set of rules

Rules provide the boundaries and we need to explain them clearly and simply and in a friendly way.

*eg 'I have three simple rules for you, children:

1 Sit down quietly when you come into the room.

2 Don't talk when I'm talking.

3 Don't get out of your seats without permission.

Thank you.'

Note the use of 'thank you'; in this case, it assumes that they will do as they are told.

Always use please and thank you with the children and then you are entitled to ask the same in return. This is the basis of the mutual respect that should form the basis of the teacher–pupil relationship. (See below.)

It is important to keep the rules simple (KIS) and always be polite. Use just a few rules to begin with. Decide which are the ones most needed by your class at this time, and when these rules are embedded you can introduce new rules as required. If you follow the guidance on reinforcement in Chapter 9, normally you will have the children settled to your expectations in a couple of weeks.

Make your instructions clear

Teachers give children a great many instructions which they are expected to follow. Instructions are directives and the important thing is that they must be clearly understood and succinct. Begin with an 'advance organiser', then work out a logical sequence and spell it out in short steps and simple language.

> ***eg** 'In a moment, children, I am going to ask you to line up to go to assembly. I don't want anyone to move until I tell them to. Table 1, stand up please and put your chairs neatly back in place, then wait quietly at the door....'.

In this sequence of instructions we have taken preventive measures by anticipating that the children may start to move as soon as they hear they are going to assembly and we have also avoided leaving the classroom untidy. This type of anticipation is usually learnt by doing it wrong in the first place and improving on your instruction technique.

If it is possible to illustrate your directive in a more concrete and visible way, then that is even better.

> ***eg** 'Here is how I want you to set out your work', and in true *Blue Peter* style ... 'Here is one I made earlier'.
>
> On other occasions you may get the children to model the behaviour or demonstrate it yourself.
>
> The object of the exercise is clarity.

Until you gain in expertise it is worth thinking through instructions and writing them down for yourself in the same careful way that you pre-prepare your rules.

chapter 9

Catch children being good

This is the basis of the behavioural psychology which reinforces a desirable action with a positive response, i.e. operant conditioning. The alternative is to remove an undesirable action by a negative response, i.e. punishment. Until the late 1970s, before corporal punishment was banned, the main strategy for maintaining discipline tended to be physical punishment, sometimes severe. The culture was mostly to 'catch children being bad'. The advice to new teachers then was to jump on the first child to step out of line and make an example of them. Thank goodness, the culture has shifted and we predominantly try to 'catch children being good' and reward behaviour that results in a reduction, even an elimination, of the more deviant behaviour.

Remember that everyone likes to be thanked and valued

This Big Idea applies not only to children of all ages but to everyone. (There is a very old saying about catching more flies with honey than with vinegar.) It is also a way of making children of all ages feel good about themselves and raising their self-esteem, (see Chapter 10). This is the main reward incentive used in behaviour management, whether it is social behaviour or academic behaviour that we want to reinforce. A smile and a thank you can go a long way. This is the *invisible* reward system compared with the visible and concrete.

It is worth commenting on the language we use to thank the recipient. Put simply, it must be age appropriate. Some of our children grow up very quickly and are 'streetwise' by the age of 10. We need to make sure we treat them more as 'young teenagers' than 'older infants', when we speak to them.

This is a very good 'people management' technique and one that the more enlightened businesses use in preference to the more 'draconian' approaches to people management. It also works with teachers, not to mention husbands, wives and partners!

Establish a mutual respect with the class

This was alluded to in Chapter 8 as the basis of the pupil–teacher relationship. Someone once told me that if you get this right children will 'walk through walls' for you. There is a lot of truth in that adage. The pupil–teacher relationship is one in which the teacher is the senior partner and the pupil is a respected junior partner. We show our respect for children not only in our pleases and thank yous, but also in our endeavour to help them achieve. The quality of our planning and preparation also sends a message to the children that you care about them, as well as the empathy you show towards them daily. Children naturally reciprocate and, if politeness is a stranger to them outside school, they will soon learn it with you as part of the 'contract' (see Chapter 10).

Respect is a two-way street and if we show this towards our children we have a right to ask for it in return.

Teachers earn it and children return it.

Only very disaffected and often damaged children fail to respond to this moral code.

Reinforce good behaviour with praise

We have mentioned this basic principle on several occasions; however, we need to look a little more closely at how we apply that strategy.

Praise is the key but it must be contingent on the behaviour you want to see and must follow it as soon as convenient. We need to make a clear connection between the action and the consequence (stimulus – response theory). On the one hand try to avoid continual interruptions to the flow of your lesson, even for praise, and on the other hand it is not very effective to wait until the end of the lesson to give praise. It needs to be done as soon as possible but not on every occasion; common sense is once again the key.

In the beginning the reward should be used more frequently. Children are quick learners and after a day of focused reinforcement of one particular good behaviour you will notice a marked difference. As time goes by and the behaviour has begun to be 'internalised' by the children, you will hardly need the rule. The time will vary, but for most 'nuisance' behaviours, e.g. not putting hands up; calling out; talking instead of working etc., 2–3 weeks can see remarkable improvements.

Tell children what you are praising them for

We must remember that if our strategy of praise is to work then children must be able to make an immediate association between the praise and the behaviour. We must be explicit; too often we use 'well done' and assume the children will know what for.

It is much more effective to tell the children 'well done' and qualify what the praise is for.

> **✱eg** 'Well done, Class 3. You are listening much better this lesson. Thank you.'

When praising individual children for good behaviour it is even more important because it tells other children what pleases you and they copy that behaviour. (This is called the Observational Learning Effect.)

> **✱eg** 'Thank you, Alan, for waiting quietly with your hand up.'
> Or
> 'Thank you, Gemma, for sharing your rubber with Sam. That was kind of you. I like that'.

The only difference between this strategy for younger children and that with older children is the language of praise and its sophistication.

> **✱eg** 'Thank you', 'Nice one', even 'Cool', may be more appropriate followed by the reason for the praise. The principles are the same.

Use visible and concrete rewards where possible

These can be very effective, especially with primary children, although they are surprisingly effective when used in a more sophisticated manner with secondary pupils. Such rewards are particularly effective with classes displaying challenging behaviour, which is often the case at the beginning of the first term. When the good behaviour becomes internalised and the novelty wears off, you can replace the overt reward system with a more sophisticated approach, but only after you have discussed this with the children.

The rewards can range from names displayed on the board, to points awarded and the famous 'marbles in the jar'. The principle of all these strategies is one where the child earns a kind of currency that can be exchanged for 'treats', e.g. 'golden time' (a short period of time where the pupils have free choice regarding what they do).

There is, however, a downside to this kind of reward system and that is if the teacher overuses it or lets it fall into disrepair; then it loses its value and becomes ineffective and even counterproductive. My advice is to keep the maintenance level of the reward system to a minimum; a complicated points system takes a lot of teacher effort to keep up to date. Further, you will need to try to ensure that the reward is available to all children and not just the higher achievers. All forms of good behaviour need to be rewarded, both academic and social.

Balance firmness with kindness

'Firmness with kindness' should be our maxim. We need to:

- Be polite but assertive;
- Insist and persist and then say 'Thank you';
- Be sincere and not sarcastic;
- Be objective, factual and succinct, with a liberal sprinkling of humour and half-smiles;
- Avoid lectures and long 'telling-offs'.

For most people it is easier to be kind than to be cruel. Kindness brings its own reward and teachers tend to repeat the process unwittingly following the operant conditioning principle which they apply to managing their children's behaviour. Among the many joys of teaching are the daily rewards and satisfactions that we receive from the children. However, although it is more uncomfortable to be firm it is just as important; even the youngest children will understand that. This is not being unkind and hurtful, as some new to teaching may think; it is in the child's interest and safety. More than anything children need security, the security of knowing the rules and boundaries and the comfort and reward that comes from that 'zone'. It is worth remembering that children are remarkably resilient and soon forget the firmness and recognise the kindness of their teacher.

Teach the 'hidden curriculum'

These are the aspects of the curriculum that are not laid down in the Programmes of Study but are equally important for children to learn in order to achieve their learning objectives. Behaviour is one aspect of the hidden curriculum which includes social, emotional and intellectual behaviours. These are often taught by teachers in a more casual way by reinforcing these good social behaviours as they go along. It is often said that they are 'caught rather than taught'; however, as successful as this may be, we need at some time to teach them. By this I mean that we identify the behaviour as the learning objective and even share it with the children. We can't rely on the casual approach; we need to teach the types of behaviour we wish to see, even though they are not in the Programmes of Study.

* eg If my children were poor at listening to and following instructions I could deliver that objective through a PE lesson, among others. In this lesson I would be praising the following of instructions more than the quality of the PE, as that would be the object of the learning.

Most of the time the hidden curriculum is learned by children along the way, often by chance. We need to decide as teachers whether this is effective enough or if we need to teach it more explicitly. This is your professional judgement and will depend on the needs of your class.

chapter 10

Enter into unwritten contracts with children

Make the contract explicit

Teachers and their pupils enter into contracts and agreements; it is just that children do not consciously recognise this concept. However, they do recognise the association of 'actions' and 'consequences', which is the game we play. These contracts are often assumptions on the part of the teacher, with the children desperately trying to guess what they have to do and say to please their teacher.

Another of the many paradoxes about children is that they want to please their teacher, not displease their teacher. For this reason it is much more effective to make your understandings, agreements and contracts explicit. Once again the secret is to focus on the positive consequences, be it an 'individual contract' or a 'class contract'. In the more challenging individual cases this needs to be spelled out and measurable and achievable targets need to be set. Negative consequences, threats and punishments are not particularly effective, especially if the children's behaviour is managed in this way outside school. (See Chapter 12.)

The actions and consequences of the **unspoken** contracts referred to above are mainly driven by the 'invisible rewards' we have mentioned: the smiles, gratitude and the affection we show the children. These contracts are the secret of establishing a positive pupil–teacher relationship.

There are also **spoken** contracts which tend to be about an explicit reward, either for individuals or for the whole class.

Golden Time. The same principles apply, i.e. both parties must be clear about the contract and it needs to be targeted and measurable in some way, even if that measure is only impressionistic:

'I think you have all worked much more quietly this week and we are going to have some Golden Time this Friday afternoon'.

Don't get too disappointed if the contract is broken. There seems to be a little devil in some children which makes them want to 'wind their teachers up'. Don't take offence and retain your sense of humour.

'Nice try, Alan, now go and sit back in your place, please'.

Build up children's self-esteem

The principle behind this Big Idea is:

Value your pupils and make them feel worthwhile about themselves.

This is about knowing and respecting your pupils, but more than that it is the 'glue' that holds the contract together. It is about children's self-esteem, about 'worthwhileness', as one gifted and caring teacher once told me.

It is a fact that many of our underachieving children have low self-esteem; they don't lack the intellectual ability to achieve, as those who write them off think. They don't feel good about themselves: the way they look, friendships, lack of academic attainment, and lack of money among other things. Children with this 'compound deficit' need more than TLC, although that is also important; they need praising as 'little people', about their qualities and appearance, not just about their work. They need carefully set 'targets' at which they can succeed, easy at first, and then leading them upwards. It is about self-improvement.

'Nothing succeeds like success' is a very true adage, but in this case it is more like a 'golf handicap'. Children need to know they are competing against *themselves* and encouraged to ignore how well the others are doing. They need to know that it is *their progress* that we value and not the fact that they are not doing as well as some other children. We need to be truthful; they know they are not achieving as highly as other children. Our strategy is to emphasise their relative improvement and praise their individual strengths in other areas.

We need to turn that 'I can't do' mind-set, into an 'I can do!' one. This is one of the biggest challenges a teacher faces and it usually takes a great deal of experience to overcome it.

As has been said before, we make our children feel good about themselves with our smiles and encouragement and children, in turn, make teachers feel good about themselves by liking and valuing us. I think this reward is the main reason for the dedication of teachers. There are few jobs where there is so much daily 'feel good' factor, despite the constant changes and bureaucracy.

Develop 'withitness'

This was a phrase established by J.S. Kounin in the 1980s. It is the 'eyes in the back of your head' phenomenon, anticipating and interceding before the event, especially with a light-hearted observation rather than a threat.

 'You seem to have lost your way, Alan, your seat is over there.'

Positioning yourself around the classroom can be a mistake if you are working closely with one child or group of children with your back to most of the other children, because you will be at risk. The general rule is always to position yourself so that you have your back to the wall and then you can keep raising your head from the focus group, scanning the room and 'eyeballing' if necessary. (Remember the arc of vision: 20 minutes past the hour to 20 minutes to the hour.) In that way you will identify 'hot spots' before they catch fire!

chapter 11

Provide a safe and secure environment

Be consistent and be reliable

The Big Idea behind this principle is to provide a safe and secure environment for your children. This means more than a warm, clean and bright classroom, although that is important too. Any person who is subjected to unpredictability and insecurity will become destabilised and their behaviour will be changed for the worse as a consequence of this. Children are no different; they need you and your classroom routine to be predictable and reliable. Some of our children have fairly chaotic home lives which do not provide this stability and it takes them some time to settle to our routines and 'become schooled'.

Establish routines

Children need to feel safe and part of that is knowing the routines: what to do, what happens next and that you are your usual 'calm, caring' self. Early Years teachers are very particular about set times for set events during the child's day and not surprisingly older children respond favourably to this even though we have more flexibility with older age groups.

Teachers can inadvertently be their own worst enemies. If we are not ordered, organised, well prepared, and consistent in our behaviour and manner, clear about our rules and expectations, and do not have reliable routines, we destabilise our children and should not blame them for the consequences.

One of the problems that occurs as a result of children moving from class to class is the different expectations of different teachers. Most schools adopt a whole school approach and policies, but the devil is in the detail and there can still be significant variance between classes.

Another of the paradoxes about children is:

They create disorganisation and chaos, when in fact they love calm, consistency and order.

chapter 12

Get children to take responsibility for their own actions

Give children choices

We try to move our behaviour strategies from the Operant Conditioning mode, which brings a more immediate behavioural effect, to one where the children have not only 'internalised' acceptable behaviour but can begin to make decisions and choices about their own behaviour and attitudes and accept the consequences.

This 'deeper intellectual' reasoning can be grasped by surprisingly young children.

✱eg 'If you decide to do this then it will mean ...'.

I don't advocate a trendy intellectual debate between the teacher and child, but we need to make the reasoning and choices explicit. With older children their reasoning is important and we need to listen and consider it. Nevertheless the teacher is the final arbiter and we need to spell out the choices, explain the consequences and in this case give the children the opportunity to make their own decision.

Be objective and factual, do not 'nag'!

Use few words and offer simple choices!

✱eg 'If you carry on talking I shall be forced to speak with you at break. The choice is yours.'

Rather than:

'How many times have I had to speak to you? This is not the first time is it? Don't let it happen again! What's your problem?'

If you are telling a child off, try to avoid the use of questions as this only invites answers from the child and leads you into a debate. You are in instruction mode not enquiry mode.

✱eg 'Alan, return to your seat . . . now.'

If on the other hand you genuinely wish to understand why this situation has occurred then ask politely:

✱eg 'Alan, would you mind telling me why you have moved.'

Give children responsibility and trust them

From the simple beginnings of choosing children to return the register, to the appointment of classroom monitors and playground 'buddies' there is a need to make sure that these responsibilities are available to all. We are all familiar with anecdotes of how the most challenging children can be transformed by their new-found self-esteem when given responsibility.

Some years ago I visited a school in inner city Nottingham that pioneered School Councils. The headteacher allowed democratic elections to the Council and the appointment by the Council of their leader. Meetings of the Council were held in front of the whole school, at first with the minimum of teachers present and eventually with no teachers present. This was one of the most challenging schools I have visited in an area of serious social disadvantage. On this occasion the boy with the most serious behavioural problems, regarding police and Social Security, was not only voted on to the Council but made leader by his peers. He was transformed and ran the Council effectively and efficiently. There is some truth in the 'poacher turned gamekeeper' adage.

This is the most obvious expression of giving children responsibility, yet the most important expression of responsibility is the one we stated at the beginning: 'children taking responsibility for their own actions'.

This is often achieved in a happenstance manner, but I would argue that it is a very important part of the 'hidden curriculum' and deserves to be 'taught rather than caught'. (See Chapter 9.)

Teach children to decide for themselves and accept the consequences.

Use sanctions with care

As mentioned before, punishment can be counterproductive and, used inappropriately, can lead to not only disaffection and resentment on the part of the child but more seriously to lying, deceit and truancy.

Sanctions are necessary, but need to be handled with care. They need to be used as a last resort and have a carefully managed series of steps.

Escalation needs to be carefully considered and announced with regret by the teacher. Further it needs to be a 'two-way street' and children need to be shown how they can retrieve the situation. It needs to move from 'a quiet word', to 'a talk at break', and eventually to headteacher and parent.

Don't use threats, especially unreasonable ones; simply explain the consequences. If you wish to inform children that sanctions may follow then at first **be non-specific.**

✳ eg 'If you persist, Alan, I shall have to take further action and neither of us wants to go there.'

If Alan does persist then you can move up another notch and specify the sanction, which should be low level at first to allow further room for escalation.

✳ eg 'If I have to remind you again, Alan, you *will* stay in at break time.'

Don't 'back children into corners'. No one likes to be embarrassed or, worse, humiliated. They never forget or forgive. If it comes to a battle of wills you may lose and the child, like any trapped animal, may very well lash out physically as well as verbally.

Always give the child choices and the opportunity to defer the action and go away and think about it. A get-out clause might be something like:

> **✷eg** 'I want you to sit there and think about this, Alan. I'll speak with you in a few minutes.'

Sanctions, like rewards, need to have value and be valued. Inappropriate use and overuse of sanctions will lead to the system becoming moribund and falling into disrepair.

Strategies will vary with the age and challenge of the children but the principle remains the same: mutual respect; teacher in charge and pupils being valued.

Children have a very strong sense of fairness.

Teaching and Learning

chapter 13

You teach and the children learn

Another statement of the obvious! However, there is a great deal of teaching from which the children learn very little and sometimes not what was intended. As a beginner there is naturally an emphasis on your teaching ability and if that is competent then the children should learn.

We must also be mindful that there are two halves to this equation and not forget how children learn, and vary our approaches accordingly. Remember what we said in our Planning section: 'Teachers don't just *do* things with children; the things they do are the vehicles for learning!'

This takes us back to the importance of 'teaching points' or, should I say, 'the point of teaching.' (See Chapter 2.)

If we get it right the children learn and enjoy it, first because they succeed and gain confidence and secondly because we plan our lessons creatively with enthusiasm and they find them interesting. It doesn't have to be 'rocket science'.

Indeed, some lessons may be very routine, even boring, and children will accept this as long as it doesn't happen all the time. However, not all lessons can be or should be 'all singing and all dancing'; if they were they would probably burn us out and the children as well.

Remember that there are two levels of teaching

I will call these 'shallow end' and 'deep end', to use a swimming pool analogy. As someone once observed, 'Most of the noise comes from the shallow end.' The deciding factor is the degree of intellectual engagement demanded by the task, which is often referred to as 'brains-on'.

'Shallow end' teaching is more about children recognising and being able to recall, knowing about rather than understanding. This is less intellectually demanding and easier to assess and sometimes that is all our tests do. This teaching tends to be more instructional and instrumental in its nature. A considerable amount of our curriculum demands this approach and this is legitimate in these cases. Knowledge and Skills are often successfully taught using this approach. (See Chapter 1.)

✱eg Spelling; phonics; handwriting; counting; multiplication tables; historical dates; names of capitals; names of plants and animals; chemical symbols . . .

'Deep end' teaching involves higher-order intellectual engagement. It is about thinking and understanding. This teaching tends to be more interactive and challenging, with intelligent dialogue between teacher and children. I don't mean 'intelligent' in the 'high IQ' sense of the word, rather in the 'sensible and meaningful' sense of the word. Understanding and Attitudes and Values are often successfully taught using this approach. (See Chapter 1.)

✱eg Creative writing; understanding literature; historical interpretation; mathematical problem solving; scientific concepts; geographical enquiry . . .

This higher-order intellectual engagement aspect of the curriculum can be taught using 'shallow end' techniques, i.e. 'learn and remember this for tomorrow', but the learning is tenuous and superficial and correct recall is often confused with understanding by teachers and testers.

Most of the education I received focused on correct recall and assumed understanding, which was not correct in my case. As teachers, we need to recognise when we need to apply 'deeper end' strategies.

Use different approaches to teaching and learning

What are the different approaches to teaching and learning? Almost every education book has a different explanation; however, the following generalisation of teaching styles gives us the overall picture.

Safe vs Adventurous teaching
Passive vs Active learning
Traditional vs Trendy teaching

It doesn't take 'rocket science' to realise that on the left-hand side you are teaching well inside your 'comfort zone' and will most likely employ the lower levels of the children's intellectual engagement. On the right-hand side you are taking much greater risks that will require more complex planning, more difficult organisation and better discipline. On the other hand, you are more likely to involve the higher levels of the children's intellectual engagement and 'reach the parts that other teaching doesn't reach', to pinch an advertising slogan.

It is obvious that the greater the intellectual challenge we wish to provide for our children the deeper and more active are the teaching approaches required. It also follows that these strategies will provide a deeper understanding of the subject matter. However, we are not saying that this is the only way to teach. As I have said before, 'shallow end' teaching is expedient and effective for much of our knowledge-based curriculum.

Once again it is the teacher's professional judgement based on the curriculum content and lesson objective on the one hand and the management needs of the class and the teacher's expertise on the other. Sometimes there are restrictions in resources or time or the plain fact that the children's behaviour is not yet ready for more active learning approaches. Children need to be taught how to learn in this way. (See Chapter 18.)

As with much of teaching, striking the appropriate balance within the parameters of manageability provides the best outcome.

Apply different strategies at different times

Continuing with the theme of 'horses for courses', i.e. different content requires different strategies and different levels of intellectual engagement, there are two variables we need to examine in more detail:

1 The demand of the subject matter;

2 The previous experience of the children in working in more active and independent ways, i.e. their readiness to work in this way.

First let's look at the subject matter:

It is common sense that straightforward factual content is most easily delivered and received in a straightforward direct teaching mode where the children are less actively involved. On the other hand, where we need to get children to explore and understand we will need some form of deeper intellectual engagement and a more active learning approach. This could be guided discovery, or class enquiry and dialogue. (See Chapter 14.)

Secondly let's look at the children's previous experience:

In many cases children are well trained in listening to their teachers and answering and asking questions. This is often the mode of operation when the subject matter is straightforward and the learning less active. However, as we progress to deeper levels of understanding we need to apply the more active techniques of learning. The mode of operation here is different, it is collegial and the children need to practise and learn how to do this.

The most important rule of working in this more cooperative manner is 'turn taking' and, secondly, 'listening and appreciating what the other person is saying' and not just waiting for a gap to jump in and say what you want. These rules of social behaviour need to be taught just as much as the intellectual behaviour we are looking for. Further, if children are to be more actively involved not only with their teacher but also with other children, then we are looking for some kind of 'group work'. (See Chapter 18.)

Begin with the simple approach and progress from there

Readiness to work in this way is important and you need to start simply, unlike me. As an enthusiastic new teacher with a science background, I decided almost on my first day in the school with Y6 to organise group practical investigations. After I had spent a lengthy lunch hour of preparation the children walked in to groups of tables full of exciting resources, like beakers of water and filters. The lesson was a disaster and nearly caused a riot. (Metre rules made better swords than measuring instruments.) I abandoned the lesson after 15 minutes and sat them back into their rows of seats and made them learn some chemical symbols from the board off by heart! The amazing thing was that my punishment of learning from the board was thoroughly enjoyed. They had been used to sitting in rows and this teaching approach for the last six years and were in their comfort zone. I was too naïve to realise that a different way of working would come as a shock to the system and would have to be introduced a step at a time.

The moral of this tale is to begin with the simple approach and work from there, taking it a step at a time. In the same way that children reach 'reading readiness' or 'working in groups readiness', teachers also have to reach the competence level to be ready for managing different teaching approaches. Practice does not change overnight: it is evolution not revolution.

Help children to make sense for themselves

Common sense tells us that the 'safe, passive' approach is more appropriate for disseminating information, procedural matters and factual recall. It is often whole class 'prescriptive' teaching and 'shallow end'. On the other hand, if we want a deeper understanding to be gained and we need children to 'engage brain', as one of my old colleagues used to tell her children, we need to employ more 'active learning' where the teacher 'does it with' the children rather than 'doing it to' the children. They need to 'explore inside their heads' and make sense for themselves, to construct meaning from what they see, do and are told (a very Piagetian concept).

The above is sometimes referred to as 'brains-on' as opposed to 'hands-on'. These two are not mutually exclusive; it is even more effective if we have 'brains-on' as well as 'hands-on'. This 'hands-on', 'brains-on' can be seen throughout the curriculum including exploratory play, Sc1, Ma1, History, Geography, to name but a few. In my opinion every subject requires 'hands-on', brains-on'.

Many children are not used to problem solving or independent working and find it very difficult to begin with. It is even worth practising the thinking skills one at a time with 'mini explorations'. We often approach primary Scientific Enquiry in the same way when we wish to improve our children's observation skills or recording skills, for example. We need to begin with mini sessions on how to start looking at a problem or considering a situation.

Where do we start? What information is given? Where do we want to get to? What do we need to find out to help us get there? Once children have learned to raise their own lines of enquiry then they are ready to move on to the procedural aspects such as gathering evidence or argument; analysing evidence or argument; interpreting the evidence and coming to some conclusions or presenting a case.

These are higher-order thinking skills and involve a progression that must be taken a step at a time, where each process needs to be practised and learned. We often assume that children will figure it out for themselves, which some exceptional children can do, but for the majority of children, teachers are needed to help them make sense for themselves. (See Chapters 16 and 17.)

Teachers use a raft of techniques to achieve this objective: they tell; instruct; coach; demonstrate; model; explain; explore with them; lead them, and at times, leave them to discover for themselves. As I've said before, it's not 'rocket science'; these are strategies that can be seen every day in thousands of classrooms. Many teachers seem to apply the right approach at the right time intuitively; in fact, the truth is probably that they are experienced and reflective teachers. Beginners need to start simply and purposefully and apply a range of these techniques to help their children make sense for themselves.

Don't conflate content with process

If we take the 'reductionist' approach to our subjects, we can divide them into two:

1   Content: Basically knowledge and understanding;

2   Process: A way of doing and thinking.

For example, Science has a heavy content of knowledge and facts, but it also has a very important way of doing and thinking. This process is called 'scientific method', but you will recognise it as the Attainment Target: Sc1 Scientific Enquiry (observing; questioning; predicting; testing; making inferences based on findings etc.).

You can find a 'content' and 'process' dimension in all subjects. There is not a subject where we don't expect our children to process information logically or critically or creatively. (See Chapter 17.)

However, it is better not to conflate the two dimensions when you are teaching.

✱eg   If you are teaching an aspect of the **process**, e.g. scientific observation skills or geographical enquiry skills, then this is your lesson objective and your teaching points will focus on this objective only. Remembering the names or gaining some understanding may also be achieved but these are secondary.

On the other hand, if you are teaching the **content** aspect of the subject, emphasising knowledge and recall, this is your lesson objective and your teaching points will focus on this objective only. Gaining some understanding of the process may also be achieved but this is secondary. (KUSA is a helpful analytical tool in this case. See Chapter 3.)

chapter 14

Guide children to discover for themselves

Give children some ownership of their learning

Progressing from the above premise of helping children to make sense for themselves, we need to move on to explore a technique known as 'Guided Discovery'. Simply put, this means:

Teachers guide and children discover.

It isn't possible to use the discovery technique all the time. Sometimes we need to tell the children the facts of the matter directly and this is entirely appropriate for many aspects of our teaching. On the other hand, we know that if we give children some 'ownership' of this knowledge they are more likely to retain and understand it.

'Ownership' in this sense means 'active involvement' in the learning, with children appearing to discover for themselves. (You'll see below why I used the word 'appearing'.)

What we don't want is unplanned and ad hoc discovery; occasionally this can be helpful, but more often than not it is confusing to the child and often to the teacher as well. We should try to avoid surprises that we have not planned for.

Plan for children to discover what you want them to learn

We want to avoid surprises and get the children to discover what we want them to discover. In order to do this we have to plan for it to be discovered. Further, if we want them to discover it we need to hide it in the first place and guide them to it. This is the simple method of Guided Discovery.

Plan; hide and guide.

We then use a covert strategy where we question, lead, prompt, even suggest, until the children 'fall into the trap' and discover what we have planted there for them to discover. It is not a dissimilar technique to that used by sales people or barristers, who persuade people by asking questions until they get the answers they want. When we have guided them successfully we congratulate them and clarify and reinforce their findings, while feigning surprise.

Use questions to guide children to your teaching points

Teachers ask dozens of questions each day, many of them everyday queries and asked almost without thinking, apparently instinctive. This is perfectly acceptable and for experienced teachers it only *appears* to be done without thought. For new teachers it needs to be more purposeful. We need to lead children down that 'learning pathway' mentioned in Chapter 2 and in this case it is a 'pathway to discovery'. We shouldn't rely on good fortune, but should plan three or four steps on the way to that goal and use questions and suggestions to lead the children there.

✳ eg   'Where have you seen something like this before, Alan?'

Or the classic:
   'I wonder what would happen if?'

Or the more obvious:
   'Do you think it would be better if we did *this* or *that*, Alan?'

What we need to establish are the questions and suggestions we need to ask by thinking about them and preparing them beforehand. This preparation is necessary for beginners, but you will soon acquire a repertoire of such questions and suggestions and the technique will become second nature.

Decide whether you are questioning to assist or to assess

Again, if we use the reductionist technique and simplify questioning, we could reduce it to two categories:

Questions that ASSIST learning;

Questions that ASSESS learning.

I hasten to add that this rather clever simplification was not mine; I read it somewhere and it stuck!

Assist questions

These are the key to leading children to discover for themselves or to discover the teaching point you are trying to make. They can be 'open' or 'closed'.

These questions are very helpful at the beginning of lessons when you are setting the context and trying to encourage children to discover the teaching points so that you can set them off to work on their own on tasks.

'Closed' questions, which have generally one correct answer, are very good for leading children to where you want to get them, as the answer will provide a clue to the next step.

✳ eg   'Who knows the name of this?'

Note that this question is specific. The question 'Who can tell me anything about this?' is not usually helpful as you often get answers that are irrelevant to the direction you wish to travel. This can completely wreck the flow and create confusion, causing the lesson to stall.

Your next leading question might be:

✱eg 'Do you know where we could find one of these?'

It could be a historical artefact or a geographical feature for example, and you wish to lead the children into that time or place.

In this way we begin to lead children to our teaching points, which we then reveal with a tinge of astonishment.

Obviously, closed questions are also very good for ascertaining if the child knows the right answer to questions of fact or knowledge. We use them in this way most of the time and this is perfectly legitimate because we need to establish what children know or do not know so that we can adapt our teaching. Unfortunately this 'quiz mentality' can pervade classroom practice just as it has done with the nation's television. This can lead to an ethos of scoring points for correct answers becoming more important than the answers that show good effort and thinking but do not produce the correct result. (See Chapter 16.)

'Open' questions, which have usually more than one correct answer, allow the child to think much more widely and search their brain for connections rather than focusing on the recall of one missing fact. This is a much healthier intellectual exercise and people who are good at making connections are often very successful problem solvers, so it is a skill worth explaining to and practising with the children.

✱eg 'Can anyone think how we could explain why we only find these in this (time or place)?'

We should emphasise to children that everyone has a brain and can think and we want to give them confidence to share their thinking with us. In this way the child can always be right to some degree and we can praise part or all of their effort and thus increase their confidence to answer and raise their self-esteem. The moral here is:

Ask children what they think and value it.

'Choice' questions fall somewhere between open and closed questions; this type of question is very effective in moving things along quickly as there is a 50:50 chance of getting the answer right. (Not rocket science!)

✳eg 'Which character in the story did you like the best, *this* one or *that* one?'

Now you are on track you can ask a more open question:

✳eg 'Why did you like that character best?'

This should take you a little closer to making your teaching point.

Assess questions

These are questions that are used to find out what the children know and understand.

They can be summative – to evaluate the learning at a particular time, e.g. end of lesson(s); end of topic; end of term; end of Key Stage etc.

Or formative; this is ongoing assessment to find out what the children know now and what you need to teach them next.

Or 'diagnostic'; this is assessment to remediate their misunderstandings, or to extend and challenge the more able.

Any assessment can apply to the whole class or to groups or to individual children; the same principles apply.

In the same way as Assist questions, Assess questions can be 'closed' or 'open' and the same reasoning as above applies.

✱ eg 'Who can name the capital of the USA?' (You could simply follow the methodology of any of the host of 'dumb' TV quiz shows.)
or
'Why do you think that $10+10+10 = 30$ gives the same answer as 3×10?'

When you have identified the learners' needs, be they individual, group or whole class, it may be worth planning a lesson or other opportunity to remediate them, rather than trying to correct them on the spot.

When you teach don't test; when you test don't teach

The moral of this tale is that when we are teaching children and trying to make our teaching points, we need to question to assist and further the learning. We are not looking for right answers, so don't keep asking for them. On the other hand, when we are trying to assess and test children, we need to question them to look for right answers and we should not be trying to teach and explain when they get the answers wrong. We should simply correct them at this stage.

If you feel you need to teach because you are finding a certain level of misunderstanding, it may be better to prepare a lesson to correct the misunderstanding or prepare some individual work for that particular child rather than trying to correct it on the spot, as was said earlier.

Don't make children struggle

If you fail to extract the answer you are looking for after two or three attempts when you are questioning to assist, then tell them the answer and move things along. Getting the right answer is not the object of the exercise. Getting a response that enables you to carry on teaching is the real objective, so don't make children struggle (see below).

It is important to remember that you don't have to question children for every piece of information you require to teach them – you are allowed to tell them.

The above is the single most important reason why the pace of the lesson slows and the flow and the learning stall. (See Chapter 15.)

(I think there is some unwritten law that beginners have been told, which says that all the answers must come from the 'mouths of the children'!)

> Struggling is very different from challenging children to think more deeply or more widely.

Teach off the children's answers

When a child gives you an answer you are looking for, try to extend and elaborate the answer back to the rest of the class.

> **✳ eg**   'Good, so what you are telling us is ...'.

This clarifies the learning and reinforces the teaching point. It can also be very helpful to further the learning and put you back on track to make your teaching point.

> **✳ eg**   'Good answer, Alan, however there is another way to ...'.

It is also useful to explain the thinking and reasoning for the benefit of the class.

> **✳ eg**   'Good thinking, Alan, tell us how you arrived at ...'.

Further, it is a technique that is useful for helping the less confident and the less able.

> **✳ eg**   'I can see where you were coming from, Alan ...'.

You can then go on to expand his answer and credit Alan with things he probably wasn't thinking. He will take the credit and it will do his self-esteem no end of good and the teaching point will have been made clear for the rest of the class and the lesson moved along (PACE).

All teachers use the children's answers in their teaching to some degree or another, but not all teachers take the opportunity to make teaching points from the answers they receive. The response; 'good answer, Alan' is charming but it doesn't reinforce the learning for Alan or the rest of the class.

As beginning teachers, you need to grasp the simple method of seeking the answers you need to hear to make your teaching point and go about this task deliberately with leading questions. The alternative is that you go around the class asking the same question half a dozen times from half a dozen different children and still get the wrong answer. Don't make children struggle; this not only deflates them but prevents you from the wonderful opportunity of teaching off their answers.

> Question children; listen to answers; expand and explain.

chapter 15

Determine the pace of the lesson

Don't talk too much

Most teachers could 'talk for England'; however, you should try to avoid this. Children can only listen for so long, even if you are a 'star turn'. Children have a limited attention span according to their age and psychological disposition. Someone once said that children could only sit and listen for the number of minutes equivalent to their age. There are bound to be variances but the advice is reasonable.

You need to keep this in mind or your lesson will get completely out of balance. It will result in an over-run at the beginning and a rush at the end with an inevitable loss of learning for many of the children.

We tend to talk a lot because we know a lot and think that we are short-changing the children if we don't tell them everything or that they won't understand unless they know everything. This is not true; it complicates and confuses, so go back to one of our first principles and KIS.

As mentioned in the previous sections, we ask too many questions and make children struggle, which also kills the pace.

Stick to the lesson objective

There is a common misunderstanding that **pace** is about the **speed** of the lesson: whereas that may be a factor, it is really the attention to the Learning Objective that determines the pace of the lesson.

As we have learned earlier:

If you ask the right questions; stick to your learning pathway; make your teaching points, then your lesson objective will be achieved with an even rate of progress.

Don't confuse speed with timing

The **speed** of the lesson is a result of how fast you go and some beginning teachers go much too slow and completely underestimate the ability of their children, while others go much too fast and overestimate the ability of the children.

There tend to be two common scenarios:

1   The beginning teacher who is very academic and can't get down to the children's level, not only because there is a mismatch between the lesson content and the children's abilities but also in the use of much more advanced and more sophisticated language. The result will be that the lesson will proceed too slowly because of confusion, or too quickly because the confusion is not recognised or, if it is, it is ignored.

2   The beginning teacher who has spent hours preparing a lesson that contains enough material for at least two lessons, and is then determined to get through to the end regardless.

Speed means that the lesson is too fast or too slow.

Timing refers to the balance of the lesson.

Timing is the time taken for each section of the lesson, i.e. the beginning, middle and end. It is about allocating sufficient time to do justice to each phase without losing effectiveness.

I used to think in terms of a 'contract' with my children.

✱ eg   'I talk; you work; I talk again; then you do some more work.'

This not only allowed me to keep on pace but also allowed me to gather, impressionistically, formative and diagnostic assessment information as I moved around the class. I was then able to interrupt the lesson at a convenient point and 'feed back to feed forward' in order to refocus on the lesson objective and give extension work to those who needed it.

Refocus on the lesson objective during the lesson

The mid-lesson feedback to the class highlighting the strengths and areas for improvement is now sometimes described as a 'mini-plenary'. Whatever you wish to call it, it is a successful strategy in re-focusing the lesson on the lesson objective. Hopefully, using this simple 'monitoring' technique we all achieve 'outcomes' by the end of the lesson and both teacher and children are pleased with themselves.

It is important to try not to mention the children by name whose work you are referring to. It can cause both resentment and embarrassment. The children whose work is rarely identified begin to resent the children whose work is frequently identified. On the other hand, children whose work is used frequently can become embarrassed at the publicity. It is known as the 'teacher's pet' syndrome and every child is aware of it. It is the work we are interested in on this occasion, not the child, so anonymise it.

＊eg 'I have seen some work that …' and then give the learning criteria you are looking for as a guide or exemplar for other children.

Good pace leads to good learning progress.

chapter 16

Make the children independent

Teach children good learning behaviours

Our long-term aim should be to make our children into independent learners and thinkers. In an era where popular quiz games emphasise the 'getting of right answers' and the internet is awash with right answers, we need to be mindful that in the twenty-first century 'asking the questions' to find the right answers – or, better still, to 'question the answers' – is equally important.

Some of us would argue that this intellectual ability is more important than getting the 'right answer'. We need to give children the tools and the processes that will enable them to arrive at their own judgements.

A recent example of the recognition of this is the emphasis on Creativity, Thinking and Problem Solving, to be found in the Primary National Strategy, 'Excellence and Enjoyment', 'Key Aspects of Learning' (DfES 0524–2004 G). It is worth noting that in the 1980s there was a national network based on Thinking, from the 'Instrumental Enrichment' of Reuben Feuerstein to the 'Philosophy in the Classroom' of Mathew Lipman. Sadly this early flower was overtaken by the Education Reform Act of 1988.

If children are to become independent, we need to train and educate them in this way of working. We need to challenge them to think more deeply and more widely. There is a way of working and thinking that children need to learn and that we need to teach. This involves the 'higher-order' teaching skills that are explored in Chapter 17.

If we look at our teaching approaches simplistically we can see a progression from Direct teaching to Instrumental and Instructional teaching, to Guided discovery and finally to Independent working.

This progression moves from a 'teacher centred' approach to a much more 'child centred' approach.

There is no single right way to teach; all approaches have value. We need to use a balance of approaches as and when appropriate, depending on the content we wish to teach and the 'readiness' of our children.

A big step on this journey, regardless of the age of the children, is to encourage them to decide for themselves, where appropriate. Start by giving them choices and the children accepting the consequences, regardless of whether it refers to their work or behaviour. (See Chapter 12.)

The above is an argument for teaching children good learning behaviours. In the next chapter we shall explore the learning behaviours we are looking for. Before we consider that we need to remind ourselves of this question:

Is it caught or is it taught?

In Chapter 9 we discussed the 'hidden curriculum' with respect to learning good social behaviours; the same argument applies to acquiring good learning behaviours. The hidden curriculum is not only social but also emotional and intellectual. Whereas we all have a good idea of social behavioural expectations we don't have the same knowledge of intellectual behaviour. This will be analysed in Chapter 17.

Teach children 'good learning behaviours' and don't just assume that they will pick them up along the way.

This is the Big Idea behind what I am trying to say. These learning behaviours range from the obvious such as listening, to the 'Key aspects of Learning' as described in the Primary National Strategy, 'Excellence and Enjoyment, Learning to learn: progression in the key aspects of learning' (DfES 0524–2004).

My contention is that we often think that children will pick these skills up as we deliver the curriculum content. There is no doubt that some children prove to be good listeners and thinkers even though we don't explicitly teach that. I would argue that, if we wish to develop these intellectual skills for all children, then it is more effective to teach them in a much more deliberate manner.

Make learning behaviours your lesson objective.

First teach children to listen and then to speak

The basic intellectual skill children need is to be able to listen. Listening doesn't mean being quiet and hearing, it is much more than that. It involves intellectual engagement, trying to make sense of what is being said. We need to give children the opportunity to practise listening and making sense, asking them what they think it means and exploring their reasoning.

We need to explain and show how that reasoning was arrived at by looking for the clues and making links to other knowledge and experience that may help them to understand.

Children need to know they are allowed to work in this way and that this is often preferred to being the first person to shout out the correct answer. Share this lesson objective with the children, make your expectations clear. Try to feed the learning criteria back to them in the same way that we give feedback about the criteria of good pieces of work when we are trying to raise standards. We are trying to give the message that this is what your thinking should look like in the same way as we say that this is what your work should look like.

It is about being consistent in applying the same good practice to 'thinking skills' as we do to the content of the curriculum.

The first thinking skill is being able to listen.

The next requirement for many children is to be able to articulate their thoughts clearly, which is what is meant by 'speaking'. It is not just opening their mouths and making sounds; it should involve intellectual engagement, where children try to make sense of what they want to say before they say it.

The second thinking skill is being able to speak.

Children need practice in marshalling their thoughts and sorting them into a logical order and then articulating them in simple clear language. We don't need to get hung up on 'audiences'; we need to give children the confidence to say what they think and why to others, be it in a conversation or a group or to a whole school.

'Speaking and Listening' is a key aspect of the English curriculum. However, we need to consider this aspect as a more general thinking skill used throughout our teaching rather than the specific NC outcomes of the Literacy Strategy. It is more helpful in this sense to think of 'Listening and Speaking'.

We need to teach children to use more precise language and thought.

＊eg Avoid vague pronouns and nouns: they, everybody etc.

Avoid non-specific words: things, cool, ya know, whatsit etc.

Ask children: What is (are) the main point(s)? Can you use fewer words? Can you say it another way? etc.

Make Listening and Speaking into a theme that pervades a half-term's work and look for evidence of the progress, the 'before and after'. It will be very rewarding to you and the children to see how far they have come. It follows the same psychological process as Operant Conditioning, i.e. when first learning the behaviour it needs to be frequently rewarded and emphasised and as it becomes embedded we can reduce the emphasis and move on to another intelligent behaviour that they need to learn. (See Chapter 17.)

Teach children to produce knowledge, not just to reproduce it

Much of our curriculum requires that children 'reproduce knowledge' correctly; not only does much of our examination system expect this, but it is also the public's perception of the role of education. We need to get children to 'produce' knowledge, not merely to 'reproduce' knowledge.

> Behaving intelligently is more a response to trying to answer questions to which they do not know the answer than answering questions to which they do know the answer.

In this way children produce intelligent responses to questions to further their line of enquiry and resolve their problems. In other words:

> Thinking and reasoning are more important than correct recall.

It is our job to teach children to behave intelligently in the same way we teach them to behave socially. Listening and speaking intelligently is a very good beginning, but children also need to know that they are allowed to use these aptitudes without fear of criticism.

Create a classroom climate where children feel free to question

Before we begin to look at the intelligent behaviours we wish our children to acquire, we need to make sure the **classroom climate** is appropriate. Children need to know:

- **It is safe to question:** All questions should be valued, no matter how stupid they may appear. Ask the child what they mean and help them explore the 'clever' aspect of their question and praise them. Very few children will ask stupid questions on purpose.

- **It is safe to risk an answer:** Praise children for trying: use the trick of asking children what they think the answer might be. This is a lot less threatening than asking: what is the answer or who knows? I may have an idea but I am not sure, but when you give me permission to say what I think, even though it may not be 'right', I am more likely to volunteer, especially if I see such behaviour being praised.

- **They have time to think:** There are times we need children to answer quickly and compete for who can get there first. This is fine for shallow low-level thinking, but it tends to rely on good recall and discourages deeper thinking and reasoning. For deeper thinking children need time. Children need to know which game they are playing, the 'quick thinking' one or the 'deep thinking' one, so tell them.

Model the intellectual behaviours you are looking for

Teachers need to explain their own thinking and show children the process and criteria they are looking for in a good answer. It is the process of arriving at the answer we are emphasising, not the answer itself.

It is my contention that all children are intellectual, in the same way that they are all 'sporty' or 'arty' to a greater or lesser degree. It is just that some children appear to be naturally better at it than others, and this may be the case; on the other hand, they may have been taught better and had more practice. In the Introduction to this book I mentioned that educationalists now recognise the power of teaching to enhance children's mental capacities.

Children can learn to be intelligent.

chapter 17

Teach children to think

Teach children to reason

The outcome of intelligent behaviours is often recognised as 'thinking', hence the plethora of publications about thinking – from Howard Gardner's Theory of Multiple Intelligence in *Frames of Mind* (1983) and the sound practical teaching advice in Robert Fisher's *Teaching Children to Think* (1990), to quick-fix tips like the *Top Ten Thinking Skills* and, dare I say, the very popular *Brain Gym*. I am not disapproving of anything that will help our children to think. If it works for you then use it, but keep an open mind. What works for you today will not necessarily work for you tomorrow. There is a wash-out effect and children can grow tired of approaches and so can teachers. My contention has always been that any method taught by a competent and enthusiastic teacher can be made to succeed. Testaments to this are the various reading approaches that have been pursued over the last 40 years.

From the deeply intellectual treatises to the commercial opportunists there is an overload of publications on the teaching of thinking. When you are overloaded ask yourself the simple question:

What do I want my children to learn?

Easier said than done when faced with all this advice and information. However, I go back to two of my adages: Keep It Simple and the 'Desert Island Discs test', which is: 'You can only take one with you, which will it be?' Then the answer to the last question would be:

The Fourth R – Reasoning,

as Edward de Bono says in *Teach your children how to think* (1992).

We need to explore in simple terms what we mean by 'reasoning'. Reasoning for me is almost synonymous with thinking. This can be reduced to three strands for simplicity, as follows.

1   **Logical:** This is the type of thinking mainly associated with Maths and Science. It is a **deductive process** where one statement or number fact depends on the previous step(s) for its outcome. You are forced to this conclusion whether you like it or not, there is no room for judgement, you have to deduce what the facts are telling you (Sherlock Holmes).

2   **Critical:** This type of thinking is associated with subjects like History and PSHCE in particular, but really pervades most of the curriculum. It is still a deductive process but here we are looking for **reasoned argument based on evidence.** Unlike the above, judgement is an essential component. You need to weigh up the case and decide whether 'it is more likely than not' based on the evidence that this is so, or that that is so.

3   **Creative:** This type of thinking is associated with Art, Design, Drama and Music, but again is used throughout the curriculum. Many of the greatest scientific discoveries have been arrived at in this way and not by pure logic and mathematics, e.g. Einstein's 'Thought Experiments'. It is an imaginative process involving lateral thinking (de Bono), and is divergent and innovative. As our American cousins say: 'off the wall' or 'from left field'!

Children need to know that there are three different ways of approaching their work and problems and we need them to be 'taught rather than caught'. We should not rely on serendipity and chance. As teachers, we should explain and explore these three strands with the children and praise the Fourth R all the time.

The following is a true anecdote:

About 25 years ago I was teaching a challenging Y6 class from a tough council estate. The children were suffering from 'death by a thousand sums' so I began to introduce some everyday maths problems to vary their diet. It was the time of Wimbledon so I set them the problem of: 'If there were 100 tennis players in this knock-out competition, how many games would have to be played to find a winner?'

I explained how to deal with the odd numbers of competitors entering the round by the use of byes. The children all began to work through the 50 vs 50 = 50 games; 25 vs 25 = 25 games etc., with varying degrees of success.

The correct answer was 99 and the few children who got it right were as expected, with the exception of David, who was a very quiet, timid boy who was small for his age and suffered from a permanently runny nose whatever the season. He definitely had some learning difficulties and was mathematically challenged. David was not within sight of anyone else who had got the correct answer, so after congratulating them and sending them off to break I asked David to stay behind.

I looked at his working out, which didn't have the seven number lines the answers to which added up to 99; he just had some scribbles and then 99. Curious and not wanting to hurt his feelings, I said, 'That was a good guess, David, or did you work it out?" To my surprise he said that he had worked it out.

He said that if there were 100 players and only one winner then there must have been 99 losers and that to lose a match you have to play a game, hence 99 games!

I hadn't thought of that logic and I thought it was brilliant and made sure he got the credit and the kudos for his brilliance.

I realise that this section on Thinking may appear to be very KS2/KS3, but if, once you have established 'Listening and Speaking', you begin to look for these three processes in younger children, you will find them and be able to encourage them in the appropriate 'child speak'.

> Logic will take you from A to B.
> Imagination will take you everywhere.
>
> Albert Einstein

Help children to behave more intelligently

As we have said, we can be aware of the three strands of thinking and illustrate, explain and explore them with our children as and when they naturally occur in our teaching. We can also emphasise them when we feel it is appropriate to apply that thinking strategy to what we are teaching at the time. However, it has been my experience that there are some common barriers to children's behaving intelligently that we need to address.

- **Decrease impulsiveness:**
  For many children we need to get them to stop and think. They need to know that this is a valued expectation of the teacher. We also need to give them a simple method to consider the situation, e.g. clarify the problem/task; make a plan; where are we going? Is there anything further we need to know?

- **Increase persistence:**
  Many children give up too easily or don't even begin. This is sometimes because they have poor self-esteem, ('I'm rubbish, me!') or they don't know where to begin or continue because the task is too difficult. Tasks need to be challenging and to extend children. This is something that OfSTED point out when they visit you, and quite rightly so, but before we get children to run we need to teach them to walk.

  At first, make the problems on the easy side to demonstrate the methodology and give them early success and build confidence. For those who are struggling, show them and differentiate by extending the task for the more able. Help, support and coach: it is not rocket science, it is sound teaching.

■ **Reduce carelessness:**
This often occurs as a result of impulsiveness or lack of concentration. We need to get children into the habit of checking and re-reading their work whenever possible. We need to give them time and encouragement so they begin to learn that this is an expectation of the teacher. I accept that there will be times when it will not be appropriate to check, in our 'hurry along' and 'test-driven' curriculum.

■ **Teach them to keep an open mind:**
This is not always a natural tendency for children or adults. We feel much safer with certainty than uncertainty, so it is not surprising that we jump to the first conclusion and stick with it. Unfortunately it encourages a resistance to flexible thinking and tends to produce closed minds.

We need to encourage 'open minds' and discourage 'closed minds'. We need to praise the good start they have made in coming to their first speculations and encourage children to consider the 'howevers', the 'buts' and the 'if you look at it another way'.

If you raise these kinds of challenges first, this behaviour will begin to be transferred to the children. Further, if we encourage them to challenge each other in this way, hopefully they will further internalise this behaviour and begin to challenge their own thinking.

■ **Encourage questions:**
Children never stop asking questions: unfortunately they are usually of the Can I go to the toilet? and What do I do next? kind! We need to model, look for and praise the questions that promote enquiry, discussion and knowledge. The flexible thinking questions above with: What would happen if? How do you know it's true?; What's the evidence? What is your reasoning? etc.

■ **Stimulate curiosity and wonderment:**
Many children lose their natural curiosity once they have been in school for a few years. They stop noticing and asking

questions: they look but they do not see. They will look at a tree, for example, but not notice that the leaves are different, that they seem to get smaller towards the top of the tree.

We need to provide the children with wonder and amazement whenever possible: from swifts migrating to Africa without once touching the ground, to amazing records from the *Guinness Book of Records*, to mysterious numbers and beautiful literature. We need to ask the 'curiosity questions' ourselves – the 'I wonder why ...?' – and hopefully the children will begin to copy our behaviour and share our enthusiasm.

Many of you reading this will recognise things that you do already. This doesn't surprise me; it is good teaching and common sense, but you need to do it more systematically and consciously. Also, you need to follow our simple maxim of normally addressing only one thing at a time.

We need to be more explicit in addressing these barriers so that intelligent behaviour is 'taught' as opposed to being 'caught'.

The two main things to remember are:

1 Create a classroom climate conducive to questioning.

2 Always look for the Fourth R.

chapter 18

Organise group
work

Train children to work in groups

Why do teachers put children into groups within their classes?

They certainly don't do it because it is easier; it is much more demanding than whole class teaching. Cooperative learning and team work produce valuable social benefits; however, research in the 1980s, by people like Neville Bennett and Maurice Galton showed not only this but also that it increased academic attainment and children's self-esteem.

The Big Idea behind this teaching approach is to

> Reduce the teacher–pupil ratio in order to facilitate learning.

Common sense tells us that the best pupil–teacher ratio is 1:1, but in a class of 30 children that is impossible. Research and experience tell us that groups of 4–6 pupils are the most effective while still remaining manageable in a cohort of 30 children. The 'quality time' between teacher and pupil greatly increases with this type of organisation and hence the quality of teaching and learning, which is the object of the exercise.

> How teachers organise their class is up to their professional judgement.

Sometimes because of the nature of the task 'whole class' teaching is the most effective method; it may also be appropriate if the class is new to you and is particularly challenging.

On the other hand, the nature of the task may require cooperation, as in topic work, or be enquiry led, as in problem solving, where you want the children to work together to succeed.

It may be more effective to teach a new concept or method to a small group at a time, or it may be an effective means of differentiation, i.e. by putting children into ability groups.

On other occasions we only have enough resources for one or two groups at a time, so we don't have a choice. At times I have divided the class into two large groups working on different tasks and found that to be a good first step for both me and the children.

*eg Group 1: Creative Writing (self managed).

Group 2: Science Investigation (teacher managed).

There is no particular right way; we need to make a judgement between manageability and effectiveness. My advice would be to begin with the type of class organisation that both you and the children are comfortable with and progress from there, but be eclectic.

Children need training in group behaviour just as you have trained them in class behaviour. It is the same methodology: make your expectations clear and praise the behaviour you wish to achieve.

What are these 'group behaviours'? Common sense tells us that we want children to:

Share; take turns; listen to each other and help each other.

Many of these types of behaviour run counter to children's natural instinct, so we have to replace their natural instinct with the new types of behaviour we are looking for. Cue: Operant conditioning!

There is a good overview in the 'Key aspects of learning,' p, 54. 'Social skills' (Primary National Strategy, DfES 0524–2004 G).

All our previous experience tells us that if we are to succeed we need some 'rules' about listening to each other; not interrupting; taking turns; helping each other etc.

Depending on the age of the children you can set down clear 'rules of engagement' or suggest, and involve the children in, coming up with their own rules. As has been mentioned before children have a strong sense of fairness and having ownership will increase their fair play. It also makes an appropriate PHSCE lesson and provides a good example of a life strategy of how to start to make order out of chaos. It is worth practising the rules as separate 5-minute exercises the week before so that it is not completely new to the children when it comes to the real thing. Take things a step at a time and get it right.

Make the rules and train the children.

Teach children to cooperate

If you want children to 'work cooperatively' you really ought to set them a task that demands a common outcome.

Some tasks will mean that children will be in groups but working individually, e.g. Maths setting. If that's the intention there isn't a problem. However, if we are wanting children to work together, but they fragment themselves and work on their own, then we do have a problem. Much of the research previously referred to found that children were in fact sitting in groups but working individually.

Sharing the task out between the members of the group is a simple way of directing them to work together. After a spell of directing children to work in this way the children will model the teacher's behaviour, as we have mentioned before, and will take charge themselves and share the work out.

Decide which is your focus group for teaching

One rationale for group work is that it gives the teacher the opportunity for much more individualised teaching. It allows for much better quality teacher–pupil dialogue, questioning and explaining, which is essential for teaching new concepts or for formative and diagnostic assessment.

The problem with group work is that, in a class of 30 children, you can only be in one place at a time and you can only teach one group of children provided you are not being interrupted by the other children. When you organise the work for the groups make sure there is only one high-demand group, i.e. involved in new learning or assessment, and make this your 'focus group'.

The tasks for the other groups must be self-sufficient, i.e. they will need to know not only what to do but already be familiar with how to go about it and have all the resources they need to complete the task.

Once again go back to the principle of Keep It Simple, don't over-complicate things, begin with one group and set the rest of the class off on another task which is differentiated by outcome, i.e. start with two groups only.

Move around your groups with purpose

Obviously we don't bury ourselves with the focus group all the time; as soon as possible we move around the other groups encouraging them. It is also useful to have a teaching point in your mind for each group, so that you can reinforce a specific learning outcome rather than just saying 'well done'. It need not be a sophisticated teaching point; it can be as simple as just complimenting them on neat writing or the way they have set their number work out. There is also the benefit of the Observational Learning Effect and other children hear this and pick it up.

When moving around visiting your groups, try to have a teaching point in mind to reinforce some learning.

Help children to help each other with their learning

The reasoning behind this statement is that when children help each other to learn they go through an intellectual process which clarifies their own thinking and understanding.

Mixed-ability groups are not only very good for 'peer tutoring' and helping the tutee but are also very good for helping the 'tutors' clarify their own understanding. In this way the more able children benefit as well as the less able tutees.

The first step on my own journey of understanding teaching came after five years when I was awarded a student teacher for six weeks. In those days the University did all the mentoring and class teachers like myself regarded it as a bit of a holiday! As I mentioned, the children were quite challenging and the student's first question after his week of observation was: 'How do you do that?' He meant getting the children to sit, listen and do as they were told. After reflecting, I said I didn't know, I just did it! Pathetic, but true; however, it did begin my journey as a reflective teacher and did help me discover the advantage of peer tutoring to clarify my own understanding of teaching.

It has been my experience working with numerous teachers who mentor students that their professional knowledge is often tacit, but just like children who peer tutor, once they begin to explain their teaching to others, they gain insights themselves. This is one of the advantages of mentoring students that has been mentioned by headteachers when I have carried out school placement evaluations, e.g. 'It helps my teachers to examine their own practice.'

The above is a rationale and logic for the intelligent use of group work that will depend on the curriculum content; abilities and temperament of the children; availability of resources; time constraints; physical classroom constraints etc. The important point is that it is your decision how and when you organise your class, from direct teaching to cooperative group work. The judgement is in balancing how you expedite the learning process in the most effective and manageable way.

To conclude this section I would suggest that using the same method of class organisation all the time is tedious for both the teacher and the children and leads to stagnation.

Previous advice has been to be eclectic, but it is actually a bit more than that. You need to look at the bigger picture. You sometimes need to consider the balance of the day, the week and the half term, which is referred to as the 'rhythm and flow' of the teaching. We need to manage the demand to suit ourselves and our children: too many changes, especially in quick succession, are unsettling and exhausting; too few changes can lead to boredom.

Assessment

chapter 19

Assess and evaluate your teaching

Before we begin this section it may be worth sharing with you my understanding of the difference between Assessing and Evaluating:

Assessment is the gathering of evidence of attainment.

Evaluation is the making of judgements based on that evidence.

Critically analyse your own practice

The big question you need to address is: 'How do I get better?' In a word, *improvement*!

There are three key questions that OfSTED ask when they visit your school looking for school improvement. These are:

1 How well are we doing? (**monitoring** and **tracking**)

2 How do we know? (**evidence**)

3 How are we going to get better? (**targets** and **action plans**)

It's not rocket science. These questions evaluate the school's improvement and its capacity to improve further and can apply equally to teachers.

How do I become a better teacher? To answer this question you need to critically analyse your practice. What does that mean? It means that you look at what works and do it again and you look at what doesn't work and change it! It is called simply 'intelligent teaching'.

This is easier said than done as much of our teaching – as we have discovered – depends on tacit knowledge and is hidden from view. Sometimes when you ask teachers, 'How do you do that?' and they can't explain – they say 'I just do it' – what they are probably saying is that 'over years of experience I seem to have developed a way of working that works for me'.

How can you approach this in a less insidious and more purposeful way?

Identify your problem areas

Suppose we simplify teaching into four stages:

1 Planning;

2 Teaching;

3 Class management;

4 Assessing and evaluating.

This is a self-reinforcing cycle of improvement. We feed our evaluation findings back into Planning at the beginning of the cycle and modify and improve the next cycle.

We need to look at each stage and identify the 'hot spots' that are giving us problems and then we need to prioritise the ones we need to tackle first. Common sense tells us that managing behaviour (Class management) should be top of the list. Common sense also tells us that one stage impacts on another. If lessons are dull and not matched to the ability of the children (Planning and Teaching), then behaviour (Class management) will be affected. The opposite is usually also true; if behaviour (Class management) is poor, the learning, (Teaching) is seriously affected.

Look at the previous sections in this book and use them as a diagnostic check list and remember not to change too many things at the same time; it will confuse both the children and probably yourself.

Explain and **share** your changes and expectations with the children.

Measure your progress

We need to know that we are getting better not just because it gives us personal reinforcement – that feel-good factor that sustains us and motivates us to progress even further and accept new challenges – but also because it is how our performance is judged by others. If asked by your line manager how you are doing, a more analytical response than 'OK' is required.

What do you need to measure your progress against? In business jargon they are called Key Performance Indicators (KPIs). We immediately think of our 'measurement driven' curriculum and are naturally drawn to test results and focus our evidence on gathering these.

There is a 'rule of thumb' which states that children should progress 1 sub-level per 2 terms, on average.

(Y3 to Y6 = 4yrs = 12 Terms; Level 2b to 4b = 6 sub-levels; therefore 1 sub-level per 2 terms! QED.)

Like a lot of our statistics it looks very 'scientific' and is convincing, but like all statistical calculations there is a large margin of error and we must treat them with care. We are not dealing with a factory production line; we are dealing with children, where accurate measurement is almost impossible. Children don't follow straight line graphs but develop in 'growth spurts'. This can be for physiological reasons, e.g. there are brain growth spurts around the ages of 7, 11 and 15; or development can be delayed for psychological and emotional reasons. Notwithstanding this, it is still the *average* progress that is normally looked for.

Unfortunately the *average* can be a very misleading statistic.

A class of 30 Y5s interim SAT maths results give an average of Level 3c: at least 3 sub-levels to make up next year in 2 terms, three times the expected progress!

However, if we dig deeper and look at the frequency distribution, which is a much more helpful statistic, we find a different picture:

$$5 \times \text{L5};$$
$$10 \times \text{L4};$$
$$5 \times \text{L3};$$
$$10 \times \text{L2}$$
$$= \text{L3.3 Av}$$

It doesn't take rocket science to produce this analysis, which is far more informative than the statistical average. This analysis gives us a different direction for our precision teaching; it points us to sharpening our focus on the L3s and L4s if we are going to meet our SATs targets. That is not to say we ignore the L2s and L5s, but it does tell us that we can't teach all the class in the same way with 'broad brush strokes'.

You can see how the class progress records of each child along the assessment level spectrum for English, Maths and Science, become a very important assessment to inform your teaching decisions.

Don't forget children's emotional wellbeing

Children will work harder and be more highly motivated when they are happy and secure in the classroom. You can sense this ethos when you walk into someone's classroom, but it is difficult to measure because it is 'impressionistic'. These are the 'softer' Key Performance Indicators (KPIs), but we should not ignore them.

There are other indicators that correlate with these 'softer' performance indicators and can provide a more robust evidence base to share with your line manager.

✳ eg Low levels of behaviour incidents in and out of the classroom
or
Attendance data
or
Volunteering for extra-curricular activities and projects.

It is worth noting and recording because it gives evidence of a positive profile of your class that will reflect well in your Performance Review.

It is sometimes helpful to dig a little deeper and look at the numbers.

✳ eg Are the incidents (good or bad) distributed over several children or just one or two? Do they tend to occur at the same time or on the same day or in the same place?

Information like this can be invaluable in resolving problem situations.

'Every Child Matters' emphasises not only the 'academic wellbeing', but also the 'emotional wellbeing' of the child, so our KPIs should follow this advice. Whether we like it or not, our children's academic attainments carry greater authority with most parents and with OfSTED, hence it makes sense to monitor and check your progress here with care.

Interpret performance data intelligently

Earlier in this chapter we looked carefully at the interpretation of the 'average' statistic; unfortunately *and* fortunately we are surrounded by many more statistics. This is *unfortunate* because they can look confusing and *fortunate* because they contain valuable information.

What we need as teachers is 'intelligent accountability', which means that we need to interpret these data sensibly and respond to them appropriately to ensure our children's improvement. We are held to account for this by parents, headteachers; governors and ultimately OfSTED on behalf of the DfES.

We are submerged in masses of Performance And Assessment Data (PANDA), which can be difficult to grasp: scatter graphs; whiskers; quadrants; contextual value added data (CVA) etc. We need to remember that it is first of all improvement trends that we are looking for and secondly individual performance data, so that we can map the children's attainment across the class to inform our teaching strategies.

This information allows us to see how our children 'cluster' and how they compare with national trends from the test results. The PANDA data can now be found electronically at the Raiseonline site. This gives us not only individual pupil data, but also benchmark data with all pupils nationally and similar pupils nationally (CVA data).

We need to use this intelligence to compare ourselves with other similar schools and to *target* and *focus* our teaching to meet our children's needs. Different groups will need different inputs to move them up the levels, as we saw in the simple example earlier in this chapter. We need to analyse the areas of weakness and target our teaching and the children's learning. In two words, we need more **Precision teaching**.

Target your teaching to match the needs of the class

The essence of Precision teaching is common sense: it is the Targeting and Action Planning of the curriculum in correlation with the needs of the class.

Begin with the **class** analysis and work down to **group** analysis and then **individual** analysis of need. In other words, first look at the needs of the class as a whole; there may be areas of weakness by subject or within subject or areas in the hidden intellectual curriculum (Chapters 16/17), which can effectively be addressed as a whole class exercise. From there we progress to the needs of particular groups and finally we address the remaining needs with Individual Education Plans (in the informal sense). These are often for the less able and the more able children, your statistical 'outliers'. Once again, we see the 'deductive principle' of teaching in action, going from the general to the particular.

Much of our teaching is in broad brush strokes and that is appropriate as the first approach, but the evaluation of this teaching should provide us with the knowledge to apply finer brush strokes – to continue the painting analogy. This second level of teaching becomes much more precise, based more on evidence and less on trial and error. This is all about the focus and direction of your teaching which will impact on children's progress over time.

As teachers, we are well planned with long-, medium- and short-term planning. This is thoroughly professional and means that the whole school curriculum is balanced, avoids duplication and delivers the Programmes of Study. What I'm suggesting here is that we also need to look at a deeper level of planning, a level of planning to meet not only the needs of the Programmes of Study but the needs of the class. Experienced teachers do this instinctively, while as beginning teachers we are sometimes so focused on the delivery of the curriculum that we only give this a 'light touch'.

Keep a Record of Progress

This normally takes the form of a Record Book in which we list the children and capture their summative results over the year. It is the **quantitative** data such as teacher test results; interim SATs; Non Verbal Reasoning; KS1 and KS2 SATs. This information informs our judgements of the class's need. Schools also keep **qualitative** data in the form of the Foundation Stage Profile and sample exemplars of National Curriculum Levels of the children's work. This provides a benchmark to illustrate progression from Year to Year and against which to moderate teachers' Level judgements.

As a class teacher we keep our own qualitative records of children's attainment in the form of their work books, which are usually produced at the appropriate Parents' meeting. The volume of information in these books, and sometimes their condition, does not normally provide a clear picture of progress to either the parent or the teacher. We need some kind of summative picture of the children's progress.

＊eg Over 25 years ago, I taught at a school with a gifted Infant Headteacher who was ahead of her time in many aspects of teaching and management. One of the things she invented was something called a **Green Book week**, which occurred in the last week of every term. This involved a special exercise book with a green cover, carefully covered in clear adhesive cellophane with the child's name written in 'copperplate' handwriting. This was kept by the class teacher and given to the children to use in that week to put their 'best work' in. This was then marked by the class teacher and commented on by the Headteacher. It was not only a wonderful Record of Progress but also an important transition document passed from class to class and shown at Parents' meetings. It was a source of pride and motivation for both the children and the teacher. The clever thing about this system was that it was not 'labour intensive' in maintenance terms, as the children did the majority of the work, but was highly informative at an individual pupil level as it provided interval samples of progress over three years. It didn't go unnoticed that it was also a convenient way for the headteacher to monitor and track the standards throughout her school.

The fact that you can produce some evidence demonstrating trends over time will not only help you to improve and give you confidence but will also be very useful in your Annual Performance Review. There is no substitute for facts and figures, quantitative and qualitative assessments, which have been intelligently interpreted to demonstrate progress.

Don't beat yourself up

The fascination about teaching is that it is never boring. We are continually challenged: no two classes are the same and no two children are the same. That is why we find ourselves continually evaluating and reflecting on our performance, but *don't* 'beat yourself up'!

All improvement is relative. You are measuring *your* improvement against yourself. Just like the children, we all start at different points on the 'journey'; what we have to make sure is that we are going forward a step at a time.

The important questions we are trying to answer are the ones we asked at the beginning of this section.

1   How well am I doing?

2   How do I know?

3   How do I get better?

chapter 20

Assess and evaluate your children

Analyse and diagnose the children's attainments

Much of this has been said before, particularly in terms of data interpretation informing our teaching strategies. Here we need to look in a little more detail at the processes involved in achieving our evaluations.

The same three questions apply:

1 How are they doing?

2 How do we know?

3 How are they going to get better?

Monitor, evidence and **target** are the answers to these three questions.

Once again this will challenge your critical analysis. Do your records show which children are consistently failing or excelling and in which areas? Are there patterns and commonalities and do the children cluster?

We need to use the same strategies we teach to our young children in primary science and maths: sorting; grouping; looking for similarities and differences and patterns. Then we need to employ the principle of Assessment for Learning. (See p. 164.)

Once again it is a diagnostic and deductive thinking process, where we start from the 'general' and work our way down to the particular, in logical steps. Prioritise the subject, narrow your search to the area of concern and then identify the 'errors'. Are they limited to some children or the whole class? Once you have obtained this intelligence, you can begin the process of 'remediation' and decide on new teaching approaches, and plan and organise the lessons required.

Get the building blocks right before you put the roof on

Make a list of the children's needs at the beginning of each term based on the *evidence*: class records; marking; plus your *impressions* over the first 2–3 weeks, and attack *strategically*.

Some aspects may be *chronic* and *basic* and need long-term measures.

* eg Listening and speaking skills; reading interests; behaviour; cooperation etc.

It is worth noting that many of the basic deficits may not be subject focused but can be social, emotional rather than intellectual or subject deficits.

Other needs may be more *acute* and need a *blitz*.

* eg Handwriting; spelling; investigation skills (SC1; Ma1); computation; dictionary skills etc.

Note how these deficits become more subject focused, and as such, are possibly easier to deal with.

Note down the planning strategy and rationale in your 'log book' or diary; it can be useful at appraisal meetings.

Decide which are the *chronic deficits* and which are the *acute deficits*.

Analyse and identify individual problems

Once again we use the same **diagnostic** and **deductive** process to identify the problems at individual pupil level. It may be helpful here to use a 'computer' analogy to guide your thinking:

INPUT – PROCESS – OUTPUT

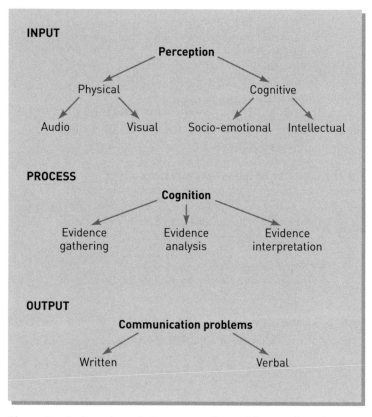

INPUT

Perception

Physical

Cognitive

Audio   Visual   Socio-emotional   Intellectual

PROCESS

Cognition

Evidence   Evidence   Evidence
gathering   analysis   interpretation

OUTPUT

Communication problems

Written   Verbal

These simple 'trees' can help narrow the problem and guide you to adapt your teaching to give the child greater accessibility to the curriculum.

Push at open doors

Identify the weakness and then find an associated strength to provide success and confidence to enable the child to move forward.

> **✱ eg** If writing is a problem but talking is a strength, then limit the writing in the beginning using discussion, then teacher scribe and pictures, and then slowly introduce *achievable* writing targets.

It may be rather a simplistic example, but it is the principle that we are trying to illustrate:

> Identify weakness; look for a compensating strength; use the latter to remediate the former.

The above is *not* an attempt to train teachers in Special Educational Needs teaching but simply to apply a little common sense and 'intelligent teaching'.

Feed back to feed forward

This is the key element that distinguishes 'assessment *for* learning' from 'assessment *of* learning', i.e. not only assessing how well children have achieved but how they can get better.

When we assess children we must feed back to feed forward (Paul Black *et al.*), i.e. tell the children how they can improve. That's why we need to use not only the response that tells children what is good about their answer, but also how it could be improved upon. We may wish to elicit how they think they could improve, but in the end they need clear guidance and expectations and that is our responsibility.

Traditional marking comes in a variety of forms, but in general it simply measures how one child has achieved and usually compares that with the other children. The reward is mainly praise and/or the ubiquitous 'gold star' or its equivalent. This has a great deal of value and provides encouragement to the child, but we also need a more intelligent form of marking. As we have said above, we need to feed forward and this will need to be focused on the specific rather than the general. What is the specific? Look no further than your learning objective and mark against that.

Here is some common sense advice that may be helpful.

*eg

1   Try to look for what the children have done well: highlight three or four examples and **tell them why**.

2   Try to identify **one** aspect that the children could improve on and **show them how**.

3   Don't overcomplicate and demotivate children by introducing
    other improvement criteria that may need remediation;
    note these down for later, e.g. If you are marking a piece of
    creative writing, award the marks for creativity and feed
    back on this and not the spelling.

This advice works not only for individual feedback but is also
very effective for whole class feedback. It is often more efficient
and manageable to identify the common strengths and
weaknesses of the work in question and prepare class feedback
which addresses this without naming individual children.

Professor Paul Black and Dr Dylan William at King's College,
London, are leading researchers in this field and Shirley Clarke of
the Institute of Education, London, gives good practical guidance
on her website (www.shirleyclarke-education.org).

Be systematic and be methodical

Gather evidence about your children's progress in the most efficient and effective way.

After all, this is the main Performance Indicator on which the headteacher and the parents will judge your success. I would argue that it is in your interest to gather this information yourself rather than to leave it to internal or external tests administered to your children.

Assessment is about reflecting on your progress and the children's in a **systematic** and **methodical** way. You can look at a range of development of your children, not just academic achievement, but the 'emotional wellbeing' of the child also needs to be recognised. On the other hand, happy children with poor attainment results will not impress parents or the headteacher or OfSTED.

Don't make the process too bureaucratic. Keep the systems concise.

A Record Book should inform your practice.

If you are filling in record sheets to please your tutor or headteacher and not examining and analysing them further, you should seriously consider why you are doing this. Lists of results are fine but they need interpreting and annotating. Use coloured highlighters to pick out patterns and anomalies. Make brief summative comments about what they are telling you and aides-mémoire of what actions you need to take.

Impressionistic assessment by teachers is valuable.

Throughout the day teachers receive and process hundreds of impressions of their children's work and behaviour. The problem is that these tend to be rather ephemeral and disappear in the 'hurly burly' of classroom interaction. Rather than just absorbing as we move around the room we also need to reflect later and be a little more analytical and note the patterns, similarities and differences in a more conscious way than we perhaps do at the moment. This often tells us things about our children and our class that we didn't suspect.

It can also be useful to be more proactive in your impression gathering. Since you are the teacher you already know the specific learning criteria or behavioural criteria, you are looking for, so look for that specifically. In other words, 'Have they got it?' This is something teachers do all the time, but usually in a more episodic rather than a methodical way. Once again focus on looking at specifics rather than the general and in that way it will seem more manageable and less overwhelming. Both casual observation and focused observation are valuable in their own right.

chapter 21

Personalised
learning

Try to personalise the learning

Throughout this section we have referred to looking more deeply from class analysis, to group analysis and then to individual analysis. This is the first step towards personalising the learning and sometimes only as far as we can go. As with many other things we have observed about teaching, there is a 'readiness' factor. Children have to have reached the level of maturity and received the training necessary to work in this way. Chapters 16 and 17 are vital in this process and, unless this foundation has been laid, personalised learning becomes the privilege of the very able.

> Children will learn a lot better if what they are taught matches what they need and they have some ownership of their learning.

In 'A Vision for Teaching and Learning in 2020'(DfES 04255-2006DOM-EN), much is made of the change in pedagogy that will be required in the future. It emphasises **personalised learning**, which it describes as:

> learner centred;
> knowledge centred;
> and
> assessment centred.

It further emphasises the need for children to take 'ownership' of their own learning. On page 20 of the above DfES document there is a helpful cycle of the three key components in this process of taking ownership:

Learning how to learn:
developing the skills
and attitudes to
become better
learners.

Assessment for Learning:
coming to a shared understanding
of the learning goals and how
to achieve them.

Pupil voice:
Establishing the habit of
talking about learning
and teaching and
how to improve it.

The document talks about using data to inform teaching; drawing attention to small steps in learning; focusing on higher-order thinking skills; cooperative group work; curriculum flexibility and Topic work; open-ended tasks; and teacher–pupil dialogue to encourage children to explore their ideas through talk, not to mention the role of ICT.

This seems to reflect what this book is all about.

Develop independent lifelong learners

I take some satisfaction from the fact that my vision of Big Ideas about Teaching and Learning is in harmony with the findings of this Government Review Group. In fact, we share the same Big Idea:

> We want children to enjoy and value their education and develop into independent lifelong learners.

This is the last Big Idea but probably the one that encompasses all the others.

Epilogue

In closing this book I should like to wish you the best for your chosen career. My advice is: when things may seem to be 'getting you down', always go back to the reason you entered the profession:

It is about children and 'making a difference'.

Finally, I should like to leave you with some philosophy that has been doing the rounds for at least 20 years. Its origin is unknown to me and I know it's very 'touch feely', but there's a great deal of truth in it. See what you think.

Children live what they learn

When children live with criticism,
They learn to condemn.

When children live with hostility,
They learn to fight.

When children live with ridicule,
They learn to be shy.

When children live with shame,
They learn to feel guilty.

When children live with tolerance,
They learn to be patient.

When children live with encouragement,
They learn confidence.

When children live with security,
They learn to have faith.

When children live with fairness,
They learn justice.

When children live with praise,
They learn to appreciate.

When children live with approval,
They learn to like themselves.

When children live with acceptance and friendship,
They learn to find love in the world.

(Author unknown)

Index